**Books are to be returned on or before
the last date below**

For Norman, who started it all,
and Jamie Magnus, who waited until it was finished.

CLEMO
— A Love Story —

SALLY MAGNUSSON

A LION PAPERBACK
Tring · Batavia · Sydney

Copyright © 1986 Sally Magnusson

Published by
Lion Publishing plc
Icknield Way, Tring, Herts, England
ISBN 0 7459 1230 3
Albatross Books Pty Ltd
PO Box 320, Sutherland, NSW 2232, Australia
ISBN 0 86760 854 4

First edition 1986

Printed and bound in Great Britain by
Cox and Wyman, Reading

Acknowledgements

I would like to thank Jack and Ruth Clemo for allowing their lives to be scrutinized and some of their most intimate memories probed and filleted for public consumption. There were a few areas where my journalistic curiosity had to be sacrificed to their request for privacy; but my intention from the outset was less to produce a detailed biography than to chronicle an extraordinary love story, and in that I always had the Clemos' full co-operation.

Anyone who wishes to delve further into Jack Clemo's life will find a personal account in two volumes of autobiography, *Confession of a Rebel* and *The Marriage of a Rebel*, both of which I have plundered shamelessly in the telling of this story. Where I quote Jack directly in the pages that follow, the passages are taken either from those books, or from his other published writings, or from my own recorded conversations with him and his wife.

My questions to Jack were laboriously transcribed onto his hand by Ruth, using the palm-writing technique that they have perfected over the years; his answers came in long, type-written replies. Ruth's side of the story emerged in successive interviews, with useful background to her teenage years in Weymouth supplied by John Murphy's book *Dorset at War*. Most illuminating of all were their love-letters, freely laid at my disposal and yielding a fascinating insight into the progress of their relationship both before and after marriage.

My thanks go also to the many local people in the claylands, neighbours and contemporaries of Jack, who helped me to form a picture of his early life at Goonamarris. I remain particularly grateful to the late Maurice Glanville, who received me with the grace and charm for which his friends will always remember him. A special thank you to Rev. Jock Stein of Carberry Tower in Scotland for his encouragement.

Finally, I must say a special thank-you to the staff of the maternity unit at Wexham Park Hospital in Slough, who put up with me and my typewriter for several weeks and helped ensure that my other production was safely delivered the day after this one.

Sally Magnusson

The publishers gratefully acknowledge permission to quote from the following works by Jack Clemo: *Confession of a Rebel* published by Chatto and Windus; *The Marriage of a Rebel* published by Victor Gollancz Ltd; *The Invading Gospel* published by Marshall Pickering; *The Bouncing Hills* published by Truran. They would also like to thank Jack Clemo for permission to quote extracts of his poetry, and Charles Causley for permission to quote 'Homage to Jack Clemo' published by Macmillan in Causley's *Collected Poems*.

Contents

1

The Road to Goonamarris

On Sunday the twenty-third of June, 1968, the world was still reeling from the assassination of Senator Robert Kennedy; the yachtsman Alec Rose was heading back to Portsmouth on the last leg of his single-handed sail round the globe; and on the Cornish clay-dumps the lupins were out.

Ruth Peaty, walking a shade hesitantly along the country road to Goonamarris, found the splash of yellow a relief. The lumpy expanse of grey clayscape on every side was beginning to get her down. It was as grim-looking a place as he had warned her it would be, and she had to admit she was feeling a bit on the grim side herself just at the moment.

Less than a mile ahead of her lay what was bound to be the most momentous meeting of her life. However it turned out, she had the feeling that nothing would be quite the same ever again. She wondered for the umpteenth time what on earth she was doing here, miles from home, about to meet for the first time a man she was practically engaged to but had never once seen.

She knew that she would see him in a moment or two. He, of course, would not see her, because he had not seen anybody or anything for about thirteen years. And she wouldn't be able to speak to him, because he was deaf as well. But don't think about that, Ruth, she told herself. Just keep going.

It occurred to her that there was something oppressive about the way the past had clung to this place. There must be generations of rust on these bits of discarded machinery that littered the roadside at her feet and protruded awkwardly from among the weeds on the clay-dumps. Here were the weird clay-lands that Jack had written so much about—the entrails of an industry that had devoured his grandfather's farm, supplied his

9

father with a meagre livelihood and haunted his own imagination so relentlessly as to provoke some of the most disturbing poetry she had ever read.

Here too must be where his parents had courted, skirting the clay-mountains on their weekly walk in the gloom of evening over half a century ago. It was that wooing that had led, in the strange way of things, to her own unlikely romantic pilgrimage today: a Weymouth laundry worker on her way to meet a deaf and blind poet who believed that his destiny was to marry.

Yes, it *was* a little unusual. She smiled to herself wanly. But then, Jack Clemo was an unusual man, and theirs had been an extraordinary love-story right from the start.

2

The Promise

It was the chapel choir that had really started it all, some sixty years before Ruth Peaty set out on the road to Goonamarris. Reggie Clemo was something of a dandy with a swagger to his walk and a ring on his finger, and he loved singing. So did Eveline Polmounter, a fifteen-year-old farmer's daughter who sang contralto to his baritone and thought he was quite the most handsome man she had ever set eyes upon. Every Thursday evening after choir practice they took to walking home together around the clay-pits with the chords of Wesley's hymns still pounding in their ears, bathed in a musical glow which blinded them to the fact that they had little else in common.

Eveline was the last of twelve children born to John and Jane Polmounter on Goonvean Farm. Six had already died before she appeared on the scene, and one of her surviving brothers emigrated to America while she was still very young. She was the child of her parents' middle age, the baby of the family. All her sisters were many years older, except tiny Bertha, only three years her senior, whose growth had been badly stunted by premature birth. Eveline always remembered her parents as elderly people with white hair.

The Polmounter tenant-farm was right in the middle of Goonvean clayworks in the heart of Cornwall. Today china clay is a vast, mechanized industry, dominating the area for miles around St Austell. But in John Polmounter's day it was still competing greedily for land with rural Cornwall, gradually eating up the ploughed fields that blocked its expansion. The landowners sold the land happily enough. They could make more in compensation from the clay-barons than they ever got in rent from the tenant-farmers. So, as his farm diminished year by year, John Polmounter put his horses and carts to use hauling coal and clay from one section of the nearby works to another, and from the works to the nearest port. A horse could earn a good deal more than a clay labourer in those days.

Goonvean Farm was one of the last agricultural outposts. There were still fields around it, almost in defiance of the clay industry, and it even boasted a little orchard. You could look out towards the moors around Meledor and imagine you were miles out in the countryside. But those fields sloped to the rim of a plunging clay-pit, and pressing in on the other side of the farm-house were drying-sheds and a railway siding. The horizon was beginning to assume the bizarre appearance it has today, bumpy with mountains of discarded sand and quartz, like some eccentrically misplaced Alpine range.

Young Eveline led a sheltered life within the green circle of fields and orchards. She was a dreamy, sensitive girl, naive, steeped in worthy religious books and cheap romantic novels, with little interest in the lives of the clay labourers beyond the farm. Her only contact with the world outside was on the days she accompanied her father on preaching expeditions. John Polmounter was a Methodist lay preacher who used to sally forth every Sunday, resplendent in long white hair and beard, to one of the little village chapels. He was a big exuberant man, well liked and respected in the district. His farm yielded little, but he was famous for his compulsive generosity. Wherever he saw poverty worse than his own, he gave. His home was cheerful and God-fearing, and Eveline enjoyed what she later came to think of as an idyllic childhood.

She was the last sort of girl, people thought, to be likely to fall for a fellow like Reginald Clemo. The Clemos were one of those unfortunate families for whom nobody had a good word. They lived in a cramped cottage almost encircled by towering white rubble from Trethosa clay-pit and were desperately poor. On a clay labourer's pittance of a wage, John Clemo had to pay his rent and feed and clothe eight children. But what alienated the rest of the community were his bouts of drunken violence. The village of St Stephens was rife with stories of his mad rages and public brawls. Some nights he would return from the pub and drive his wife and children from the house, leaving them to wander in all weathers around the white sand-tip looking for shelter in the workmen's huts.

It was little wonder that his wife Esther, a striking woman with a strident voice and frizzy hair dyed brown, gave up on domestic pride and allowed the overcrowded little house, thick with clay-dust and grime, to sink into squalor. The children were allowed to run wild.

Their son Reginald developed into an attractive young man. He struggled hard to escape the social stigma that clung to the Clemos. He had no more money than anyone else, but used what he had to dress with flair, cutting a singular dash in the neighbourhood with a bow-tie and hat. The ring he sported on his finger was an unprecedented frivolity in a down-to-earth working class community. His own son was later to describe him as a man possessing a great deal of charm, but with a streak of surly brutality simmering not far below the surface.

By day Reggie worked as a 'dry-man' at Trethosa clayworks, toiling long hours for a paltry wage in the oppressively hot kilns where the clay was dried. But in the evenings he liked to dress up and step out, to enjoy the admiring glances of the local maidens.

Perhaps it was his desire to drag himself out of the mire of his home-life that reinforced Reggie's decision to join the Trethosa chapel choir, which was led by the local coal merchant, Irving Minnear. Reggie had never evinced any particularly devotional tendencies, but he did love to sing and his rich baritone was warmly welcomed at the chapel. The choirmaster clearly had no idea what he was setting in motion the day he placed John Polmounter's bonny fifteen-year-old daughter with the contraltos, right next to the baritones.

Young Eveline was bowled over. She was as shy and introverted as Reginald was cheeky and outgoing, but their Thursday evening walks back from choir practice soon drew them together. The Polmounters looked on aghast. A Clemo boy was not the

13

partner they would have chosen for their youngest daughter. But they let the couple alone, hoping the fancy would pass, and were greatly relieved when eighteen-year-old Reggie announced that he was going off to seek his fortune across the Atlantic.

Full of hopes, he set sail in 1909 for the copper mines of Montana in the Wild West. He settled in Butte City, where he dug copper ore in an Anaconda mine, working down the shaft like the tin-miners at home in Cornwall. Sometimes, to earn a bit of extra money, he helped out in a ranch in the area, and sent home a photograph of himself posing dramatically in cowboy garb, revolver in hand. It was a rough place, and although Reggie never spoke much about his life there, he seems to have found it hard to resist the frontier spirit, where the work was hard but the drinks and the girls were easy. He never forgot Eveline, though, who was now in domestic service back home in the village of Foxhole. Just after her sixteenth birthday he sent her an engagement ring in the post from America.

Reggie arrived home in 1912, twenty-two years old, no richer but presumably a good deal less innocent than when he left. The following year he and Eveline were married at the Methodist chapel in St Austell. They moved in with her parents at Goonvean Farm and Reggie was soon rising early to help old John Polmounter to feed the livestock before going to his old job in the kiln at Trethosa clayworks. On 26 November, five months after their marriage, Eveline gave birth to a baby girl, who lived only five weeks.

The baby's death was the first blow in a marriage which was never very easy. Eveline, overwhelmed with grief at the loss of their child, craved an open affection that Reginald seemed unable or unwilling to offer. From what their son Jack wrote later, their temperaments seem not so much to have clashed as to have failed to touch each other. While Reginald was extrovert with a still roving eye, Eveline was by nature retiring and contemplative, deeply religious. It is impossible to predict how their marriage might have turned out after its uneasy start, for just when Reginald seemed to be settling down to domestic life, the

14

First World War broke out. He went to Woolwich to work in a munitions factory and was later transferred to Devonport dock-yard, slipping home at weekends whenever he could.

In 1915 his father-in-law, John Polmounter, died and the farm passed into new hands. Reginald and Eveline were offered one of a group of small clayworkers' tied cottages on Goonamarris Slip, a few hundred yards east of the farm which by this time had all but disappeared into the omnivorous Goonvean pit. They moved there at the end of the year, piling the Polmounters' heavy Victorian furniture on to a waggon which creaked its way slowly up Goonvean lane to their new home. Eveline's widowed mother, Jane, and her tiny deformed sister, Bertha, went to live with them.

It was a plain granite cottage, dwarfed by the mountainous clay-tip looming behind it. Downstairs there was a kitchen for cooking and sitting in, and a back-kitchen behind, dominated by a fireplace which was straddled by an enormous grate on which the big iron boiler could be set on wash-day. They put most of the furniture—an old sofa, an arm-chair and an organ—into the kitchen in an attempt to make it feel more like a living-room.

Upstairs the two small bedrooms were damp and musty, but each boasted a view which spoke volumes about this strange corner of Cornwall. From the back bedroom you could see nothing but the chimneys belching smoke at Goonvean pithead, the ground littered with machinery and rubble, the scene unremittingly grey. But outside the front bedroom it was different. There the last of the countryside still flaunted itself. There was a little wood where bluebells bloomed in spring and hedgerows promised to burst with autumn berries. The cottage on Goonamarris Slip commanded the frontier between the old world and the new.

And that was where Eveline gave birth to a baby boy on 11 March 1916. Little Reginald John Clemo bounced vigorously into the world, as strong and healthy as his sister had been frail. His parents called him Jack. But Reginald senior had little chance to get to know his son. Early the following year he was called up and joined the Navy as a stoker. In the summer he was drafted into active service aboard the destroyer H.M.S. *Tornado*. It was torpedoed off the Dutch coast just before Christmas. On Christmas Day 1917 Eveline received a telegram from the Admiralty. Reggie Clemo had not been among the survivors.

Eveline was crushed. While Reggie had not been a perfect husband, they had grown closer of late and she found the agony of his loss hard to bear. She was left with an aged mother, a handicapped sister and a baby to look after, in a damp cottage with only her widow's pension to support them, together with savings of £80 that Reggie had left her. In her distress it was the quiet Methodist faith that had nourished her childhood which sustained Eveline now. She prayed, as she recalled many years later, for strength to carry her cross bravely for the sake of her child. She resolved to pour all her energies, every ounce of her love, into giving her son the best possible life she could offer.

But one blow followed another. She had lost her little girl and then her husband—that was bad enough—but within two years of Reggie's death, she lost her mother, Jane, who, despite the infirmities of old age, had been her greatest support. Eveline began showing signs of a nervous breakdown and the doctor sent her and Jack to Newquay to recuperate.

They were hardly home before she had to face another crisis. Young Jack had given her no worries until now. He was a quick child, flabbergasting the neighbours at eighteen months by reciting the Lord's Prayer from beginning to end without a hiccup. He was reading voraciously by the age of four and was generally acknowledged to be brilliant, if a touch 'forward' for these parts. It was just a few days before his fifth birthday that it all started to go wrong.

Jack began to complain of pain in his eyes, and his mother was shocked to see a film over his right eye. The local doctor diagnosed it as iritis, a disease that affects the nerve endings of the eyes. The specialist at Truro said the only way to save the child's sight was to keep him in darkness for several months.

It was a desperately frightening time for the child, spending his fifth birthday swathed in head bandages, fearful of the blackness, and in such a panic when his mother tried to put the eye-drops in that she had to wheel him to the doctor's surgery two miles away every evening to have it done there. The road was rough, and older members of the community remember to this day the sight of that gaunt figure pushing the bandaged child in his chair up the bumpy track in the twilight, day after day.

Subsequent trips to the hospital at Truro revealed little improvement. Jack describes them as 'a hazy nightmare in the depths of my mind'. In *Confession of a Rebel* he paints an extraordinarily vivid picture of those visits: 'I could see nothing until I entered the doctor's consulting room where the bandages were taken off and I discerned vague shapes of furniture, a stabbing blur of light, two indistinct figures, the specialist and my mother, talking about me. The doctor would pull my eyes wide open with his thumb and finger, rapping out a continuous "Look at me! Look at me!" while I struggled to face the light and stare into the strange flickering countenance, my mind blank and rigid between panic and stupor. Then the cloths were tied round my head again and in renewed darkness I would be led out and down into the city, to the bus, holding mother's hand desperately, knowing nothing of what she suffered. I would sit beside her on the homeward journey, tired and fretful, hearing the purring of the engines, the crisp chatter of voices outside the black wall that surrounded me.'

At home Jack was almost hysterical with fear and his mother found the strain nearly unbearable. In her agony, it was a promise that sustained her. 'I have never forgotten the distress I went through at this time,' she wrote in old age. 'It seemed as if all my hopes had been dashed to the ground. I felt I could not face life with a blind child and no husband to help carry the burden. My human weakness gave way under this strain. One day, in an agony of spirit, I went to my bedroom and, taking my Bible in my hand, I knelt by my bedside praying to God for light in the darkness. Opening my Bible, and casting my eyes on the

17

page, the first words I read were "Fear not". These two words gripped me and, as I continued to read, I received an unforgettable promise.'

The promise she received that day was to lend Eveline Clemo immense courage and dignity throughout the years of struggle ahead. The grit and determination shown by a woman known to everyone as gentle and retiring were much remarked upon in the district. From those earliest years people wondered how she ever managed to keep going, and her answer was always the same. It was the assurance she had received that day by her bedside from the words of Isaiah: 'Thy children shall be taught of the Lord, and great shall be the peace of thy children.'

It was almost a year before the first attack of blindness passed. When the bandages were at last removed, Jack's sight was clear but he had changed. Gone was the lively, chattering little fellow who had liked nothing better than to show off for the neighbours. Jack emerged from his cocoon silent, sullen and moodily introspective. He showed an interest in nothing and nobody. His mother hoped fervently that starting school would help, and not long after his sixth birthday in 1922 she enrolled him at Trethosa Council School, over a mile away from his home.

Jack hated school. From his first day there to his last, he was a misfit. Lessons bored him. He had a quick mind when a subject interested him, but very little did. While his classmates were competing eagerly to answer a question or darting out to the blackboard at the invitation of the teacher, he remained rapt in a dream, with no inclination to learn and even less to join in the team spirit of school life. He must have exasperated his teachers, because it was clear that underneath the sluggish indolence of his demeanour there was a sharp intelligence that they were powerless to activate.

Only in English composition did it flash out. The infant teacher was so impressed by his very first piece of writing that she took it to the headmaster, who promptly read it out to the older class with the admonition that they ought to be ashamed to write another essay after hearing this one by a boy of six. Throughout

18

his short academic career Jack continued to win praise and prizes for his essays, one of the first being an award from the National Canine Defence League for a composition about dogs. One of his old Cornish class-mates still remembers those early Clemo essays. 'When the rest of us finished,' he said, 'Jack would still be writing foolscap paper, and the next day he would be out in the front of the class and it would be read out to the class all that he wrote. And he used words that baffled the schoolmaster.'

The only other part of the curriculum that stimulated Jack's imagination was religious study. The hymns and the Bible stories that he had learned on his mother's knee possessed then, and retained throughout his life, the power to stir him as little else could. He loved morning assembly—the songs, the prayers, the readings—which had the other children wriggling with impatience. But that didn't help much with his sums. His end-of-term reports were full of suggestions that he try harder at just about everything, notably arithmetic, geography, science and history. Doing some homework, it was noted pointedly, would help.

The headmaster, Mr Pellymounter, struggled manfully to understand the boy. He reckoned Jack's literary aptitude could take him far, but his hopes were dashed one day when he discovered that Jack's sole ambition on leaving school was to be a sky-tip worker—the man who emptied the refuse-waggons at the top of the huge clay-dumps all around the school. You could see one of the tips from the schoolroom window, watch the tiny figure working at the top and hear the rumble as each load of sand was knocked out of the skip. Jack used to gaze out at the Trethosa tip, dreaming of the solitude and the freedom he would enjoy up there, away from people and children and the demands of classroom and playground. Mr Pellymounter made a joke of Jack's ambition at the time. A year or two later, when his wayward pupil was about to leave school at the age of twelve, he told Mrs Clemo that her son was a born philosopher.

Jack's schoolmates were less charitable. The other children had little time for the kind of boy who preferred the loneliest corner of the playground, not out of shyness, but out of an impenetrable reserve. Jack was an utterly solitary figure, who shied away from every sporting or team activity, partly from profound loathing, partly from physical weakness. He was forever absent with colds and chills, a small, thin, pale child who looked for years as if he would never survive the winter.

One schoolmate remembers him as 'a reserved, frightened little boy whom you didn't pay a lot of attention to. He was always going and being sick.' Another says his image of Jack Clemo is of a figure standing alone while the rest of them were in the school-yard or the nearby field, playing football or rounders or cricket. He remembers exactly how Jack looked in those days: 'He was dressed in black leather leggings and black boots. And those leggings were absolutely shining. You could see your face in them (that was his mother) and in the boots too. And he also wore—oh, he was well groomed—a tie. Very respectable and everything in place. And he had black hair, and his hair was well combed over. He had a side parting in his hair.'

Predictably, Jack was the source of much childish derision. Even the teachers called him by his playground nickname, 'Jean'. Every half-hearted attempt to join in with his fellows failed. As he reported later: 'I made two appearances as a public entertainer during my childhood—once when I sang a solo at Trethosa chapel anniversary, and once at a concert given at the day-school when I took part in a negro sketch. I failed to impress anyone but mother on either occasion.'

Jack was happiest out of school. He loved escaping at lunchtime across the clayfields to his grandmother Esther's cottage, the home where his father had been brought up under Trethosa clay-dump. His mother would meet him there with a packed lunch and he used to wander about the garden till she arrived, waving to him from the skyline as she picked her way down past the clumps of furze, basket over her arm, to the house halfhidden below.

The claylands were Jack's playground. He loved to scramble

20

over the quarry and clamber among the empty, rusting clay-waggons on the slopes. In other moods he would just sit still for hours, dreamily contemplating the landscape that one day would invade his adult poetry. It was a wild-looking place, and Jack's home on Goonamarris Slip was on a particularly remote and inhospitable ridge of land, nicknamed Vinegar Point because of the sharp winds that regularly blasted it. Neighbours on the Slip were cut off from each other by rubble-strewn quarries and pools of water, and from the surrounding villages by rough lanes that were difficult to walk.

To this day the hills of waste-clay, as familiar to Jack Clemo as the Lakes to Wordsworth or the Yorkshire moors to the Brontë sisters, are quite simply like nothing on earth. Some look like creamy beach sandcastles deeply etched with rivulets, as if a child had poured water down their slopes. Others are more like an old wrinkled face, every line beaten into it by years of exposure to the elements. Here and there you can still spot a railway track winding its way to the top where an old waggon perches at a rakish angle, as if it has just unloaded its cargo and is waiting for the sky-tip worker to send it down the rails again for another load.

Long-abandoned quarries have attracted green lagoons of rainwater, their rims strewn with bits of pipe and wheel and ladder, a broken chimney here, the rust-chewed hulk of an excavator there. And all over the place, wherever a pit is worked out and the centre of modern operations has shifted, Nature has begun to reassert itself. A luxuriant jungle of vegetation has crept over the neglected works. Thistles and brambles and ferns and nettles have commandeered the old sluices and made their home among the fragments of railway track going nowhere. It is as if Nature has hurled itself into overdrive.

From earliest boyhood Jack watched it all happening. He saw the claymaking process rip up the countryside and impose its own industrial rhythms on the land, then move on to another patch when the pit was exhausted, leaving weed and insect to reclaim their own. Many of his poems would reflect the cycle of activity

21

and neglect that he observed as the years passed. In 'The Flooded Clay-Pit', for instance, he would muse:

> What scenes far
> Beneath those waters: chimneypots
> That used to smoke; brown rusty clots
> Of wheels still oozing tar;
> Lodge doors that rot ajar.
>
> Those iron rails
> Emerge like claws cut short on the dump,
> Though once they bore the waggon's thump:
> Now only toads and snails
> Creep round their loosened nails.

When Jack was a boy, he could still see the countryside, now utterly over-run by clayworks. In summer he and his mother used to roam the woods beyond the front of the house, gathering berries for fruit tarts. There was hay-making to watch in the remaining fields, and sometimes he would help Mrs Clemo with the gardening in the little patch of flowers which it was her delight to cultivate near the house.

In the evenings he fetched water from the pump along the road or, when that ran dry, from the claywork spring in the valley below. He or his mother collected milk each day from Morcom's, the nearest farm. The winter evenings saw him trudging out with a wheelbarrow to collect furze, or rather the burned furze twigs known as 'smutties', to save money on fuel. He and Eveline also kept their eyes open for the cinders that often carpeted the Bloomdale dump behind their home, tossed out from the engine-house above.

'I would sometimes climb fifty feet up to reach the newest layers,' Jack has written, 'crouching ankle-deep in the black ash, glancing down at mother as she waited beside the bath among the shadowy bushes, the stacks of Goonvean growing dim across the fields behind her, the clay-pit remote and melancholy. The

22

beauty of the scene was an enrichment that prevented me from ever feeling humiliated or degraded while thus grubbing in the dirt.'

There was nothing degrading about the way that Jack and his mother lived in those days, despite their poverty. They lived simply on her pension and a small war orphan's pension for the boy. Local people often left them gifts of garden produce to help out. They knew times were hard for the family, and Mrs Clemo was much respected for the dignified way in which she bore her troubles. She was immediately identifiable in the district—as the woman in black. She always wore a black, or very dark, dress, a black coat and a black hat—never a colour. Some folk were cruel enough to ridicule her way of dressing, but more were awed by the quiet strength she seemed to exude as she went about. She never possessed much, but she always believed that God would supply her needs.

Eveline was careful to ensure that Jack and her sister Bertha had enough to eat and warm clothes for the winter. She was determined that Jack's childhood would not be deprived. She used the £80 that Reginald had left to make sure that her son had toys for Christmas every year. He still remembers the joy of waking up on Christmas morning to see a green wheelbarrow by his bed, filled with parcels. He was at his happiest sitting indoors with his mother of an evening, snug and safe, playing draughts or ludo at the kitchen table. He had a meccano set, too, and a magic lantern.

Sometimes they entertained each other on the old organ that had been brought from Goonvean Farm. Eveline used to sit under the pale light of the oil-lamp, accompanying herself as she sang Sankey hymns out of a tattered copy of *Sacred Songs and Solos*. Jack, listening intently beside the fire while his Aunt Bertha knitted silently in the corner, grew to love those hymns. He never lost that early fervour for the music and the rhetoric of revivalism, believing always that the fiery tub-thumping gospellers—even when they were sentimental—represented more truthfully the essence of the Christian faith and spoke more powerfully to the soul of the worshipper than the religious rationalizers would admit. Jack, too, learned to play by ear; he never did master musical notation, but he improvized the Sankey tunes and bashed them out with good heart.

His mother maintained the religious atmosphere of Jack's early home life by reading aloud, especially on Sundays, from the books of sermons and evangelical biographies that John Polmounter had left behind. Jack's mind, so wholly unreceptive to adventure stories and schoolboy classics, lapped up the pieties of his mother's chosen reading matter. They suited the dreamy, mystical cast of an imagination harnessed from babyhood by the intensity and simplicity of Eveline Clemo's faith.

Harnessed, it's fair to say, but not tethered. Mrs Clemo was wise enough not to limit the boy's reading when he began to explore further and though she must have had qualms later on when she saw the way his tastes developed, she rarely tried to censor him. When he was about ten she scraped enough money together to buy him all the volumes of Arthur Mee's *Children's Encyclopedia*, which provided him with much of the general knowledge he disdained at school. It also introduced him in a cursory way to poetry, of which he read as much as he could find. Thomas Hardy's he liked especially, and he was greatly moved one day in 1928 when he happened upon a scrap of newspaper reporting the poet's funeral. He had already begun to feel a vague sense of kinship.

That piece of newspaper wrapping carried one of the few snatches of outside news that penetrated the Clemo household during Jack's boyhood. They couldn't afford a daily newspaper, did not possess a radio and went only once to the new-fangled cinema in St Austell. That was when Jack was twelve. The outing was never repeated, so shocked was Mrs Clemo by the 1928-style debauchery on screen. The little ménage at Goonamarris lived in a state of isolation, both mental and geographical, so thorough that you would have thought there required nothing to complete it.

But for Jack at least there was a much more profound isolation

24

to come. Although its immediate effects were temporary, it brought his schooling to an abrupt and permanent halt and ended, in a sense, his childhood. A few weeks before his thirteenth birthday, eye trouble struck again.

3

The Romantic Vision

The new attack of inflammation and semi-blindness did not last as long as the first one at the age of five, but it proved equally traumatic. The bandages went on again; there were more long, tense visits to the eye specialist at Truro and Jack retreated once more into the darkness. At first he seems to have experienced something akin to relief: he was free of school. He had longed to be alone and now he embraced his enforced solitude with a somewhat perverse pleasure. When schoolmates came to the cottage to visit him and bring him news of lessons and sports, he barely spoke to them, leaving his mother to sustain the embarrassed conversation.

But the relief did not last long. The feel of the bandages around his eyes—several layers of white linen with thick green cloth between—soon began to irritate him. He felt stifled by the binding of the cloth around his face all day long and it bred in him, he says, a kind of horror. In desperation his mother found an alternative. She settled him on a board which she fitted daily in the recess under the stairs. It was dark, very dark, and for several weeks Jack perched there like an animal, his eyes unbandaged but every other part of his body appallingly constricted. Beside him was a small cup of boracic lotion and a wad of cotton wool, and every so often he would bathe his eyes to ease the inflammation. For hours on end it was the only movement he made, except at meal-times when he emerged from reverie to pick up the plateful of food that his mother deposited on the board beside him.

It is hard to imagine what it would feel like for a young boy to be confined like that for weeks on end in the darkness. Its effect on an already hypersensitive child like Jack was profound. His reaction was not to fight the blackness, nor to waste much energy on resenting his plight. Rather, he embraced it. He crept closer and closer into himself, thinking, wondering, asking why this should be happening to him, what it all meant. With his mind as free to range as his body was imprisoned, he swam deeper and deeper in a sea of introspection. All the brooding, internalizing tendencies that were by now natural to him were reinforced in these weeks above the stairs. At thirteen, the boy conquered the terrors of blindness by cultivating the mind of a mystic. Much later, by the time he had reached his sixties and was in the grip of permanent blindness, Jack would be able to shrug off its influence by asserting that it was not part of his real life; the spiritual world was the reality. That mental victory began here, above the stairs at Goonamarris.

But the immediate effects of the experience, coming just at the dawn of adolescence, were hardly promising. The first thing his mother noticed when Jack's eyes had improved enough for him to leave his shelf was that he had become more reclusive and anti-social than ever. As she wrote later: 'When this second attack of blindness passed I saw another change developing in his temperament. He became restless, morbid, slovenly in his appearance, he would not conform to convention and gave up going to chapel.' The years that followed this experience were undoubtedly deeply troubled.

There was, though, one immediate new interest. Just before the bandages were removed, Jack was taken to a female cousin's wedding nearby. There he was greatly flattered by the attentions of the groom's sister, a twelve-year-old girl called Evelyn who took it upon herself to look after the unseeing lad, leading him by the hand to the wedding breakfast, stroking his hair and whispering softly to him throughout the meal. The effect on a boy whose senses and emotions had been so starved was electric. That day was born an obsession that was to haunt his imagination for a long time to come.

He could not get the girl out of his mind. With his poetic temperament, it was unlikely that Jack's feelings for Evelyn

27

would be anything as simple as a mere infatuation. She had come to him as a vision when he was blind, and ever afterwards he connected her appearance to him at her brother's wedding with the dawning of his artistic creativity. As his sight improved, he took to climbing Bloomdale clay-dump behind his home and gazing out wistfully from the summit towards the village of Nanpean where Evelyn lived with her parents and sister. It was in these moments, he says, that he felt the first stirrings of a desire to write.

Evelyn, in a way that was both ridiculous and yet wholly serious, was Jack's earliest inspiration. Not that she ever inspired anything particularly sublime. His first literary effort was something he denounced later as 'a crude, sentimental love-story', though it thrilled him at the time. His mother was rather less impressed. She had been a little taken aback when he suddenly put it to her not long after the Evelyn 'vision' that he might become a writer. 'What about if I was to write stories,' he had blurted out one day, 'like . . . like they 'Ockings?' (The Hocking brothers were distant relatives who had achieved a certain celebrity with sentimental tales of dubious literary merit but wide popular appeal.)

Whatever else she had dreamed of for her son, Eveline Clemo had never seen him as a literary man—although she was beginning to wonder what on earth he possibly could do for a living. His health was much too weak for him ever to become the free-breathing sky-tip worker he had once yearned to be, his solitary nature made him shy away from a light job on the clayworks where he would have to mingle with other labourers, and his sight was too poor for a job at the Treviscoe Co-Op. His orphan's pension would end when he was sixteen, and she knew their financial future was precarious. But a writer . . . ?

Still, when he proudly produced his first story and she saw that he was in earnest, Mrs Clemo swallowed her doubts and threw herself behind him with the same devoted enthusiasm with which she had applauded his soot-streaked performance at the school concert and which she would continue to pour unstintingly into

28

all his efforts—good and bad—throughout her life. She copied his story out neatly for him on several sheets of paper and sent it off to the only publishing outlet she knew, a weekly religious magazine. She was almost as crushed as he was when it winged its way back again with all speed.

Jack's next literary effort was more successful. After discovering some old copies of a Cornish annual called *Netherton's Almanack* on top of the dresser, he decided to try his pen at the kind of mildly humorous sketches in Cornish dialect that the *Almanack* appeared to like. He found the stories came easily. He had a good ear for dialect, and those tales of his that have been collected in a volume called *The Bouncing Hills* reveal a zest for slapstick humour that might not be suspected from the sombre introspection of much of his work. Later in life, when he had found security and happiness, Jack would be able to release a sense of mischief that was not much in evidence in the early years; but in those youthful stories the clues were there. He drew on observations from his childhood, weaving sometimes laboured comic yarns out of incidents half-remembered, conversations overheard. The editor of the *Almanack* liked them, and paid him half a guinea a time, his very first earnings.

Jack was overjoyed when the first one was accepted, and even more so when the opportunity arose to inform the maiden he regarded as the romantic inspiration of his budding literary career that he was now a published author.

More than a year after her brother Harry's wedding, Evelyn's parents invited Jack and his mother to Nanpean for Sunday tea. Jack, who had had no contact with the goddess since that day and had never yet actually set eyes on her, met her in a state of profound agitation. What he saw was a plump brown-haired thirteen-year-old with not very much to say for herself. Nevertheless the vision remained intact and as soon as he was home, he sat down to write a short ode in her honour. He called it 'Dreams of Yesterday':

O dearest maid, my long-lost love,

My heart still cries for thee,
For the low sweet music o' thy voice
Like the low deep throb o' the sea.

(*Refrain*)
I know it's no good wishin'
For what can never be,
But I just can't help a thinkin'
O' those happy days wi' thee.

His mother was highly suspicious when she read it and remained blankly unimpressed by explanations about 'inspiration'. When he earnestly showed her the account of Dante and Beatrice in the *Children's Encyclopedia*, which he thought paralleled his own experience rather neatly, she remarked darkly that 'Dante didn't marry her'.

Loyal as always, Mrs Clemo put aside her doubts about the moral propriety of lyrics about dearest maids with voices like the low throb of the sea and supported his next attempt to get it set to music. They had seen advertisements from music publishers looking for new talent, and on enquiry one firm offered to publish Jack's song for a fee of £15 — a fortune in that household. Mrs Clemo had £20 left of the £80 left by her husband, and she had planned to eke out the remainder over many years to come. But now, knowing his heart was set on it and hoping it might lead to greater things, she raided £15 and sent it off. When the song appeared in 1931, fewer than twenty copies were sold and she received a mere £2 back from the investment. After this, Eveline Clemo was going to take some convincing about the value of romantic inspiration, Dante or no.

Nothing daunted, however, Jack ploughed on. Keeping her misgivings to herself, his mother accompanied him on several more strained and bashful visits to Evelyn's home, visits which always stimulated a flood of literary activity back at Goonamarris. He burned the oil till past midnight, sitting at the kitchen table with the lamp at his face, straining to see the words that danced feverishly over the pages of his exercise book. He was now working on a short story which became a long story about romance in the Rocky Mountains. It ended, he recalls, with a girl confessing to the heroine that she was going to have a baby. The story kept him busy for several months and was read by his mother with fortitude.

Before he was fifteen, he also began firing off letters to the local newspapers. This activity became something of a career over the next few years. His first few letters were innocuous enough. If eyebrows were raised at his earnest argument in the *Cornish Guardian* that boys of fourteen should read love stories instead of thrillers, no one could take exception to an epistle of which he was equally proud: one detailing the finer points of his dog Gyp for an edition of *The Tail-Wagger* magazine.

His mother was so delighted to see him in print that she couldn't keep it to herself, and soon the news of Jack Clemo's embryonic literary career was all over the district. One person who heard about it was a Trethosa man called Sam Jacobs, a leading Labour Party activist who had been Jack's Sunday School superintendent. He offered to do what he could to further the boy's ambition, and when Mrs Clemo told him that the main problem was making Jack's work pay, he suggested a course of tuition in the kind of writing that would sell. When he learned that they could not afford the fees for a correspondence course (the money had been blown on the ill-fated 'Dreams of Yesterday'), Jacobs badgered the Ministry of Pensions into making Jack a grant so that he could take a course in short story writing with one of the London schools of journalism.

This did not prove a success. Jack's temperament was totally antipathetic to set exercises and the kind of writing to a marketable formula that the course demanded. The subjects that his tutor suggested—office romance, sport, hotel life—all left his imagination cold. Jack was deeply engrossed in Victor Hugo's *Les Miserables* at the time and wanted to write on the grand scale. He also insisted on giving everything he wrote a religious

31

flavour. His distracted tutor pointed out that this was all very well, but did people normally quote the Bible at each other in the middle of a passionate embrace, and did he really think that sort of thing would sell?

The course ended in the autumn of 1933 with little to show for it except a pile of encouraging correspondence from the tutor, urging him not to give up, and one extremely practical aid to his writing career. This was a typewriter, a big black monster of a thing which his tutor had persuaded the Ministry of Pensions to donate. Jack composed on it for decades.

The typewriter was called into immediate service in the frontline of Jack's increasingly controversial campaigns in the letters page of the *Cornish Guardian*. For a long time these letters of his, gloriously self-important as only an opinionated teenager can be, constituted his sole published literary output and as such assumed a huge significance in his life. Many of them are hopelessly pretentious and touchingly innocent in their adolescent bravado, but at the time, in a small local newspaper with not much else to get excited about, they provoked the sort of stir in which Jack revelled.

The week after Christmas 1931 he informed his readers: 'I believe—sincerely believe—that until a child knows the full facts of sex, it cannot grasp the full significance and therefore the full enjoyment of Christmas.' Without this knowledge, he suggested, children miss out on the miracle of a child entering the world. And he ended, with all the pomposity that his fifteen-year-old pen could muster:

> This letter may reveal me to your readers in a new light. My previous letters on immoral novels and the recent Armistice celebration have, I fear, given the impression that I am a thoughtless and flippant modernist. May this letter correct that fallacy.
>
> JACK R. CLEMO
> Goonamarris, St Stephens, St Austell.

This brought an elderly retired evangelist by the name of S. E. Burrows into the fray. He wrote with laboured irony:

> Sir—I am wondering whether your correspondent, Jack R. Clemo, is not taking himself just a trifle too seriously . . . Of course, all of us ought to have known this high doctrine before: that our little ones must know all about sex before they can understand Christmas . . . I notice that he hopes by this precious effusion to remove a fallacy as to his being regarded as 'a thoughtless and flippant modernist'. Personally, I am more disposed to regard him as a priggish, self-inflated dogmatist, who has tried to look clever by putting on his grandmother's horn-rimmed spectacles. This is bad for the sight—things get blurred!

The pair battled on happily, and with a good deal of behind-the-print respect for one another, for years. Jack's most consistent theme in the columns of the *Cornish Guardian* was his theory of the interaction between sex and religion, which in more considered form became the cornerstone of his later thinking. At this stage his prime motive was to shock, something he managed successfully early in 1934 in a series of letters provoked by the collapse of his courtship of Evelyn. In one, he announced that his 'pathway to the stars was along the little, despised, twilit trail of sex'. Whatever that might mean (and coming from a youth whose lurid imagination was only matched by the most virginal inexperience in matters amorous, it didn't mean very much), enough people were scandalized to satisfy him.

At the end of the letter, he added a few lines from a poem he had just composed. These declared that he, the poet, would

> 'Arise to let men know
> That Christ's own face can glow
> In love's embrace, and kisses be as prayers.'

Much of his later poetry explored precisely the same idea, but the lines provoked Burrows to accuse him of having 'a sex-poisoned imagination'. Correspondence on the subject raged for months, until Cornwall's most eminent novelist, Daphne du Maurier, wrote to complain that it was lowering the tone of the newspaper. She dismissed Jack, and quashed all further debate, in one crisp sentence:

> We are not interested in his views, religious, political or sexual, and if he wishes to express them let him do so in private correspondence and not before our eyes in print.

The teenage years are a difficult enough time for anyone, but for Jack it was harder than most. He had stumbled into adolescence straight from the mental horrors of the stairway recess, cut off from normal youthful pursuits by a combination of temperament, handicap and geography, and struggling to accommodate all the powerful new stirrings of puberty within a particularly sensitive and self-aware psyche. Little wonder that his thinking in those years was confused and his behaviour so strange that his mother was near to despair.

He wanted as little to do with youngsters of his own age as he had at school. His contemporaries recall that Jack never joined the gangs of boys and girls who used to gather for walks and a stolen kiss or two up on the St Dennis road. As one of them said: 'It was the same thing at our Methodist Church tea treat. We would finish up in the field about half past ten, quarter-to-eleven, playing the kissing rings in twos and threes, and we'd end up walking a girl home that we'd got friendly with that day. But Jack went home with his mother, see. Jack was out of all that. He was a student type of boy, shy, isolated. Girls didn't go after him. But Jack was seeking for that sort of company all the same.'

Jack shrank from the collective conviviality of mass gatherings and his nature recoiled at anything so gross as casual kisses on the St Dennis Road. Instead, he did a great deal of thinking and immature writing about sex; and, at the same time, sublimated his sexual energies in the fantasy pursuit of Ideal Beauty in the shape of young Evelyn from Nanpean.

In the summer of 1931, he had hit on a great plan for visiting her more often. When Evelyn's married brother Harry offered him a ride in his milk van one day, Jack was delighted to discover that Harry always stopped on his round at his parents' home for a cup of tea. Jack too was invited in, and for nearly a year after that he accompanied the milk van on its travels several mornings a week so that he could stop off and see Evelyn on the way. He reports a significant rise in literary activity at this time.

The arrangement came to an ignominious end when the local housewives began to complain about all the coughing he was doing among the milk. Standing out in all weathers at Foxhole every morning, waiting for the van to arrive, had not done Jack's health much good. When the housewives protested about the germs he was spreading, Harry was forced to withdraw his welcome and Jack had to return to more conventional ways of seeing his beloved.

Visits to Evelyn became more and more strained. She suffered them with barely concealed hostility, either ignoring his conversation or listening with frigid politeness while Jack read aloud from his latest manuscript. Eventually she took to departing just as he arrived, leaving him to spend the evening discussing the finer points of Pauline theology with her father. It is little wonder that Evelyn had no time for him. As Jack wrote later: 'She had seen me grow from a gentle, intelligent boy into a wayward and repellent youth who was somehow obsessed with her, yet not in love with her.'

And 'repellent' is the right word. Throughout his teens Jack cultivated the pose of rebel against as many conventional forms of behaviour as he could think of. He refused to wash or comb his hair for days at a time, and his mother sometimes had to sit him down and shave him herself. He would refuse to dress up for visits, or if he was made to wear a collar and tie would try to score a point by wearing them to bed. In company he indulged a stubborn clumsiness, knocking furniture over or grasping a piece

35

of cake in such a way that it fell to pieces on the table-cloth. In speaking, he came to affect a broad Cornish dialect, as incomprehensible as he could make it. All in all, as he says himself, he did his considerable best to look and sound like the village idiot.

Why? His explanation is that he was 'swallowed up in a perverse egoism that rejoiced only in humiliations and indignities'. It is almost as if his reaction to adversity was to say 'OK, if that's what you think of me, just look at how unpleasant I *can* be; just see how low I can sink when I really try!' But according to Jack, there was also a deeper reason. He was conscious of 'an acute, gnawing disharmony', which was intensified by what his mother revealed to him at the age of sixteen about his father.

Eveline Clemo was worried to distraction by her son's behaviour. Particularly upset by his latest whim (he was currently and vociferously championing free love and what he called 'sanctified smut'), she decided to tell him for the first time about his paternal family background. Jack remains reticent about what exactly his mother did reveal on that occasion.

But it is probably safe to assume that Mrs Clemo, afraid of the unhealthy direction in which her son seemed to be moving, painted him a picture of what real squalor was like and warned him of the dangers of sexual excess. Jack, whose public references to his father are always vague to the point of opacity, will only say that his mother revealed 'the ugly secrets which she had kept for nearly twenty years', and told him 'the squalid story of the Clemos and my father's tragic disharmonies'.

Whatever he did learn in those conversations with his mother, it clearly sank deep into Jack's soul. In time it became central to his understanding of a redeeming faith; he needed a God who could cancel out a 'stain' in the blood, who could conquer his heredity and revolutionize his nature. The savagery of some of his later poetic images—an excavator ripping out sin from the human soul, for instance—is more easily understood with the realization of how very personally he felt the clutch of original sin on his own life.

But that was in the future. His immediate response to his mother's revelations was, characteristically, to indulge further the very traits that she had been hoping to modify. He now realized, he says, that he had 'sprung from a family that produced more than its share of moral degenerates, and only when my habits and appearance conformed to this degradation did I feel at ease, self-contained, not divided.' It was a time of deep unhappiness and bewilderment.

All this time Jack was searching restlessly for a creed that could accommodate his complexities. He had stopped going to church with his mother by now, partly to annoy her and partly because he thought he was more likely to find what he was looking for in a Sunday roam among the clay-tips, alone with his New Testament, than in a pew at Trethosa chapel.

'I did not doubt Christianity—I merely disliked it,' he wrote much later; 'or rather, I disliked its façade, while being conscious that behind the façade there was some tremendous secret which I could not get at but which was the only thing that could satisfy me. The reasoned defence of the faith could not meet my need. I was indifferent to prosaic evidence; I demanded only an appeal to the primitive awareness that was making me a poet.'

A church which to him seemed bent on milking a supernatural faith of all traces of supernaturalism could do nothing for him. He stayed away, and his first intimation of that primitive appeal for which he was looking came quite by accident. Following Evelyn one evening, he found himself in a tiny chapel which he had never visited before away up on the moors. Evelyn had gone there to sing in the choir. He went with the idea of worshipping *her*. Instead he found himself drinking in from the service itself 'the sort of beauty of which I had been starved and for which my whole nature was crying out.'

It was an evangelistic service, strong on emotion, resounding with the old Sankey hymns that brought back memories of winter evenings in childhood with his mother pounding the organ in the lamplight. The handful of folk who made up the congregation— 'old women who twiddled their thumbs and old men who rocked

37

themselves and squeezed their eyes shut as they sang'—all looked as if they believed what they were singing. Perhaps, he thought, the old orthodox beliefs were the real ones after all. As he wrote later: 'I had come to that building ostensibly to court a girl; I left it filled with a great love for primitive Christianity, for these sturdy believers.' He was so moved by the experience that he forgot all about Evelyn and went home without speaking to her.

The service left a deep impression on him. It gave him a sense of emotional assurance, the feeling of being on the right track at last, although it would be some time yet before he arrived at the insight that would finally solve his problem. That was the perception, as he says in *The Invading Gospel*, that 'the ultimate step towards Christianity is not a search but a surrender.' But for the time being he was still too busy with his entirely unhealthy obsession with Evelyn. In the end it was she who forced him out of it. Fed up with being followed to choir practices and pestered ever more rudely at home, she returned the handkerchief and the bundle of photographs that he had given her as presents. A letter from her mother to his made it clear that in future no further visits were to be allowed. Evelyn was going to look for a job in domestic service in St Austell and would rather not see or speak to him ever again.

Jack's first reaction was the defiant bravado of the 'twilit trail of sex' letters to the *Cornish Guardian*, which he hoped she and her mother would read and be shocked by. Then he slumped into black despair. Evelyn's rejection marked the end of a nightmare, the final collapse of the 'romantic vision' in which he had invested six years of emotion. In time he would feel cleansed, but at the moment he was numb with the pain of it.

It took one more trauma to complete his misery. A few months later his mother began to notice that he was answering her in a more than usually stupid fashion, and before long she realized it was because he couldn't hear her properly. By his nineteenth birthday, he was too deaf to take part at all in a conversation, and with mounting alarm Eveline took him to the ear specialists at a hospital in Plymouth where he was given an X-ray. The results so devastated her that she could hardly bring herself to tell Jack what the doctors had told her.

This blow towards the end of his adolescence was even harder to bear than the loss of his sight on the threshold of it. That had proved temporary. This time Jack was told that there was little prospect of his ever being able to hear again.

4

Wimpole Street

For three months Jack lived in a kind of stupor, in which people glided around him like ghosts and the dog's soundlessly barking jaws haunted his imagination like some grotesque parody of his own fate.

Then he realized that he was beginning to be able to distinguish voices far away through his right ear. It was a welcome respite from utter stone-deafness, a thousand times better than that frightening blanket of absolute silence. But conversation remained impossible; the voices were too muffled for him to make out words. Communication was only possible with scraps of paper.

He might have found this new affliction easier to bear if life had looked more hopeful in other areas. But nothing seemed to be going right. Rejected manuscripts plumped one after another on to the doormat. Short stories, essays, articles, little collections of verse, his second full-length novel—they all returned. The financial pressures on the household were increasing. Often Jack's sheets of painstakingly typed paper would come back all lined and crumpled, and his mother had to iron them to smooth out the creases so that they could be sent to a different publisher. Paper cost money. So did typewriter ribbons, and when the one he used became so worn that he could hardly make out the letters on the page, he would dampen it with a brush to make the ink last a little longer.

With the nest-egg that Reggie had left her now long spent, Eveline Clemo was grieved to feel that she could no longer provide the decent standard of comfort that Jack had known as a child. His war orphan's pension had stopped when he was sixteen and his writing was currently bringing in less than £3 a year. Aunt

Bertha was still with them, ill now with diabetes and receiving only parish relief. They were all living on Mrs Clemo's widow's pension of 26s–8d a week, and if it had not been for the low rent she paid on the cottage—£6 a year—their plight would have been desperate.

Rather than let the family suffer more than she could help, Mrs Clemo took a job at a nearby farm, helping out with the housework for an extra shilling here and there. It must have been an appallingly difficult time for her, struggling to make ends meet, increasingly worried about Jack's deafness and his seemingly endless literary failures; none of it made easier by the pall of depression and irritability that he cast over the house. She was nearly at her wit's end with him. He was behaving worse than ever now that he had become deaf, crying for hours at the least set-back, rejecting all adult sympathy. 'Deafness,' he says, 'had destroyed the last traces of manliness in my behaviour.'

Looking back some ten years later in *Confession of a Rebel*, in which he would claim to detect an artistic pattern and a divine purpose in all the struggles of his youth, Jack concluded that the value of this humiliating period was the way it forced him back, in a sense, to childhood. He interpreted himself in this way:

> I had become so perverse that contact with adult values could only increase the perversity. I had to go back to the beginning and start afresh, to apprehend everything with the spontaneity and innocence of a child . . .
>
> A path so remote from ordinary life must lead a man either to Christianity—the only system that combines a stringent dogma with an exhortation to 'become as a little child'—or to sheer idiocy. There was no room for humanist or rationalist solutions . . .
>
> How far, and in what direction, could 'reason' have taken me in my predicament? If a man's psychological life has been disintegrated as a result of blindness, if he is then barred off from normality by deafness, and if, in addition, he has a strong creative urge and is trying to write novels

41

in working-class poverty—what, according to rationalists, ought he to do? The reply would probably be that a young fellow in such fantastic conditions should be placed in the care of a psychiatrist.

And that would have been the end of the story—a very dull and unexciting end which no one would have enjoyed. God had other ideas. He placed me, during my 'convalescent' period, very largely in the care of a girl less than seven years old—and the results were astonishing.

The girl was Barbara, who lived next door—a lively, intelligent child with no playmates of her own age in the cluster of cottages at Goonamarris. She had started tripping in to visit him of a morning when her father went off to work at Trethosa clay-dump. His job was to pile sand on the spot where Reggie Clemo's old family house used to stand. Barbara would spend the day looking at Jack's books and scribbling on the scrap-paper he offered her—mostly rejected manuscripts. Jack at twenty enjoyed romping with her in a way that he had shrunk from in his own childhood. When he began writing a new novel in 1936 called *Private Snow*, he was convinced that the emotional influence this time was altogether healthier than in the Evelyn years.

This was also the time when an important new literary discovery stimulated his thinking. Jack never read books disinterestedly. He approached the world's literature, as he approached every other event in life however big or small, with the passionate demand that it interpret his own experience. His antipathies were instant and uncompromising, with no concessions to received critical wisdom. Shakespeare bit the dust when Jack could find no trace in his work of what he called 'the religious consciousness'. Tolstoy lost his appeal the moment Jack discovered that his thinking had strayed from the biblical. Dickens, Stevenson and Scott he loathed from boyhood because their attitude to love was too superficial for him, too 'polite' and refined.

Jack could never bear anything in books, philosophy, art, or indeed women, that smacked of smoothness or elegance or sophistication. He liked the Gothic, the grotesque, the rough and ready, whether he found it in the primitive energy of revivalist religion or in the sensual paganism of D. H. Lawrence. He preferred the wildness of a child to the grooming of a sophisticated woman. He could see no beauty, for the time being at least, in a flower; only in the dark brooding clayworks in the ravaged countryside on his doorstep. His tastes developed that way partly, he says, 'because I knew that I was not a child of the peaceful, teeming earth, the proud Mother, but only of the broken, ragged earth, the earth spilled out as gravelly refuse in a process of purification.' Maturity would modify some of these views in time, especially in the days when a woman called Ruth would help him to see many things in a different way, but Jack never lost his distaste for bland refinement.

So it is perhaps a little surprising to find him in his early twenties being utterly bowled over by his latest literary 'find', the work of the wordy nineteenth-century English poet, Robert Browning. What would someone like Jack, who was also powerfully drawn to the gritty pessimism of Thomas Hardy, find to attract him in the smooth Victorian optimism of Robert Browning? The answer is that he found there both a love story and his most exciting clue yet to the way to a satisfying faith.

The Barretts of Wimpole Street was being serialized in the magazine *John o' London's Weekly*, and the story of how Browning had wooed and won the frail poetess Elizabeth Barrett and snatched her away from the prison of her sick-room in London's Wimpole Street, struck Jack with the force of a revelation. He immediately devoured as many biographies of the couple as he could lay hands on, and plunged into a study of Browning's poetry, reading it in the light of what he knew about the man's life. With mounting excitement, he reached the conclusion that Browning 'alone among writers, as far as I could judge, had emerged from adolescent morbidities to enjoy a love-life in which Christian mysticism and normal human feeling

43

were ideally balanced.'

If Robert Browning could do it, then couldn't Jack Clemo achieve it also? Here at last was an author whose life had apparently reflected just the sort of pattern he hoped might evolve in his own. And he became even more excited when his mother gave him *The Browning Love Letters* as a Christmas present in 1937. Ever afterwards he thought of this as one of the 'books of destiny' that changed his life. It seemed to Jack that the phrases the couple had used in their letters to describe their fulfilled love—such as 'ordained' and 'granted by God'—expressed perfectly the idea of a predestined love-match that his own imagination was beginning to nourish.

The Barrett-Browning love story became his model. From this time on, Jack dreamed that some day a predestined lover would burst into his Goonamarris hermitage and open up the prison to which his infirmities and his temperament had confined him—just as Robert Browning had once rather more literally swept his beloved to freedom. And this marriage of his, Jack believed, would be a marriage of a very special kind. He didn't quite have the details worked out yet, and in future years he would be forced to admit that the lady was taking an unexpectedly long time about bursting in; but from now on Jack Clemo believed, with a fervour that neither progressive handicap nor decades of disappointment would ever completely extinguish, that his destiny was to marry.

Browning also had something to teach him about Christianity. 'It was in the poetry of Browning,' Jack wrote in *The Invading Gospel*, 'that I first found a clue to the basic Christian paradox, the relation between surrender and true fulfilment.' He discovered that 'the first poem Browning wrote after his marriage was one from which all temporal attachments were excluded that God might be all in all.' Jack saw Browning as the priest-lover, whose greatest moments of religious insight seemed to have stemmed from his love-life and might never have been given him if he had not married. To someone who had been hunting for years for a clue to some area of reconciliation between

Christianity and the life of the senses, this was a revelation.

What made it even more precious to Jack was that Browning's Christian surrender came when he was at his happiest. As he said: 'At that stage of my development I could not have been convinced by the religious testimony of a frustrated person. I still feel uneasy about those who "escape" into divine love because they have been denied human love. Such people sometimes become saints, but more often they seek in God what they have failed to find in human beings—something congenial to their own natures, someone to "understand" and congratulate them . . . I was impressed and challenged by a man who could affirm the transcendent love of Christ when all the lights of his earthly joy were steadfast and unfailing.'

As his mind was being nourished by Browning, Jack felt he was also receiving the emotional healing he craved from the company of the child Barbara. He was still moody and difficult at home—quite obnoxiously so at times to judge from his own descriptions of his behaviour—but her childish affection always seemed to refresh and soothe him. Although his long-suffering mother was worried that he had 'outgrown the inspiration of a girl of sixteen only to find myself in the fantastic position of being inspired by a girl of six', even she could see that somehow in Barbara's presence he became more alert and receptive. To that extent the child helped Jack's spiritual odyssey, calming his spirit as he continued to hunt the truth.

Browning was not the only writer who had something to offer on the way. Jack was studying the Bible every day and reading deeply in the works of C. H. Spurgeon, the Victorian evangelist whose writings had been so beloved of his grandfather John Polmounter. Jack liked Spurgeon's refusal 'to force divine truth into the strait-jacket of human logic.' He also immersed himself in the biographies of men like the cricketer-missionary C. T. Studd, whose life of reckless faith impressed him profoundly. What validated his example for Jack was the fact that he and Studd had so little else in common. Studd had been a sportsman, with not an ounce of mysticism in his make-up and little appreciation of things artistic. Jack realized that such a man would have had no understanding whatsoever of what Jack liked to call 'the mystical-erotic struggle' of his teenage years. 'Yet,' says Jack, 'he pointed me to its solution, for he proclaimed the one infallible remedy for all human ills—full surrender to the invading righteousness of Christ. He kindled my determination to take the ultimate gamble, hand over my natural cosmos at the frontier, and throw myself on the mercy of God which had been so utterly veiled behind the negative façade.'

C. T. Studd, Spurgeon, Browning, little Barbara, his mother—they all played their part in bringing Jack Clemo to the point of surrender. In *The Invading Gospel* Jack explains how it happened. It was, he says, a gradual process:

> I cannot recall any time or place where I made the final act of surrender. There were many moments when I gained a heightened consciousness of the marvellous change that had come to me.
>
> Often when I was out on the clay-ridges in the evenings, the tip-beams standing up like crosses in the fading light, I would bow my head and put the whole force of my soul into the lines of the hymn, 'Just as I am, without one plea . . .' I would feel the deep tides of Christian truth flooding in over the natural defences.
>
> My conversion was as evangelical as if it took place at a revivalist meeting. There was nothing vague or woolly about it—no mystical fancy or romantic extravagance. I did not become aware of an Infinite or a Whole or a Cosmic Consciousness. I believed what the Bible said about Christ and human nature, and let the collision between His grace and my own nature smash the pagan tragedy to which I had been doomed. I accepted the forgiveness of sins and the authority of the Word, that was all.

Jack continued to shun organized religion, however, for a long time to come. He believed that too many of the churches were offering a sanitized gospel, shorn of paradox and hard edges, dull and easy. He went on spending Sundays out on the clay-dumps with his New Testament, longing for the fellowship of believers but convinced that there was no point of contact at Trethosa chapel with the 'elemental vision' with which his soul now vibrated.

Then came another blow and months of acute misery, from which his evolving faith afforded no magic protection. In the spring of 1938, Barbara left Goonamarris. Her family moved to live with her grandmother at Trewoon, several miles away. Probably no one—not even his mother—had any idea of what it cost Jack to see her go. In his desolation he wrote incoherently during the day and stumbled among the clay-tips in the evenings, blinded by tears.

The grief of a man in his twenties at the departure of an eight-year-old child who made his spirits dance is less easy to understand, and to sympathize with, than more conventional heartbreak. But Jack's anguish was none the less real for all that it bewildered those who observed his violent grief. Night after night he returned from his wanderings and went to bed, and there, he says, he placed under his pillow 'the two little articles that symbolized all the sufficiency of earth and heaven that I had known: a handkerchief of Barbara's which I had found among a pile of comics soon after she left Goonamarris, and my pocket Testament, in which I had marked against suitable texts the dates on which Barbara had been specially affectionate.'

Jack was so caught up in the events of his small universe that the build-up to the most cataclysmic war in history rather passed him by. In September 1939 Germany invaded Poland, Britain declared war and the country held its breath. . . But Jack had other things on his mind. The dramas inside his own head were much more insistent than anything Hitler could offer. Even when news of the blitzing of London was splashed over the front page of the *Daily Mail*, which his mother had begun ordering in the hope of giving him an outside interest, Jack's chief concern was that it would now be even more difficult to get his books published. When the City of London was fire-bombed in 1940, his first thought was for the fate of his much-travelled novel, *Private Snow*, which was currently with a publisher who had premises in the area. In fact, the premises had been caught in the fire, but Jack's manuscript was unharmed. It was returned a week later.

The one way in which the war seriously impinged on Jack's life was in bringing a succession of London evacuees to the little community at Goonamarris, young girls sent to the relative safety of mid-Cornwall to escape the bombs in the capital. The first was a stout eight-year-old with brown hair called Irene, who moved in next door with the family who had taken over the house from Barbara's parents. Jack soon made friends with Irene as he had with Barbara, although her nature was less sunny and she often grew impatient with his deafness. Still, her presence helped to fill his emotional vacuum and he felt 'inspiration' on its way again.

In August 1940 two evacuees came to stay at his own cottage, squeezed into a bedroom with Aunt Bertha while Jack and his mother shared the other. Pat was seven and Doris ten, and they brought simple sisterly companionship into Jack's life. He could not hear their chatter, but he enjoyed the soundless bustle as they romped over the furniture and ranged freely through the house, strewing toys and comics as they went. Mrs Clemo, too, loved having children around the place; she had a quiet sense of fun and a relaxed way of dealing with them that they responded to with devotion. The cottage began to feel like a real family home.

Many a time during that autumn Jack and his mother and Pat and Doris would stand at the bedroom window late into the night, watching the searchlights on the distant coastline flicker across the blacked-out landscape. Unlike the others, Jack was never kept awake at night by the roar of German planes overhead or by the intercepting British ones from the aerodrome at St Eval. But he was sometimes woken by a light in the bedroom and would look over to see one of the children clinging to his mother in the double bed.

He remembers being conscious of sharing their danger but equally conscious of being able neither to discuss it nor to do a thing practically to help avert it. He couldn't fight the enemy, even if he had wanted to, and he couldn't join the Home Guard like those among his former school-mates who had not gone to fight abroad. That feeling of impotence sharpened his habitual sense of isolation. Some bombs did fall in the district, and in one attack four people were killed and thirty-seven houses damaged only a few miles away at Foxhole; but Jack always refused to use the air-raid shelter beside Bloomdale clay-dump, even though the horrible wail of the siren was so piercing that he could sometimes hear it faintly himself when the wind was in the right direction.

Jack maintains that he always knew he would not be killed. He says he knew deep inside that he was being prepared for something. 'I believed my vision was being perfected for artistic expression in fiction and poetry; I even believed that since the collapse of my romantic idealism at Nanpean, God had been preparing me for mature love.' Since at the time he had little to show for either, he never doubted that he would survive the war.

At the end of 1940 he carried out a laborious stock-taking of his literary progress in the past ten years. This revealed that he had written over a million words in novels and a further quarter of a million in short stories, essays, verse and letters to the press. Out of all these words, only twenty-four short stories, three articles, forty-four juvenile poems and seventy letters had been published, all in small Cornish journals. His total earnings over the decade amounted to precisely £19–0s–6d.

But the tide of failure was almost ready to turn. By the summer of 1941 he was feeling more emotionally confident than he had felt for some time. This was mainly due to young Irene, who after begging for weeks to be allowed to come and live with her chums Pat and Doris in the more relaxed Clemo household next door, had at last been allowed to move in. It was an almighty squash, but she settled happily into her new home and the couple who

49

had looked after her were free to take up their plans to move to Bristol.

Jack, too, was happy. With Irene's presence guaranteeing that special sense of joy and comfort that certain children could bring him, he felt that his new source of inspiration was secure. He was ready to embark now upon the book that at long last would bring him a measure of literary recognition, the novel which would give mature artistic expression for the first time to his longing for a wife.

5

The Weymouth Evacuee

That same summer of 1941 found Ruth Peaty dodging bombs in Weymouth, darning socks for the Navy, and not giving any thought at all to husbands. She was eighteen years old and these were exciting times. She had arrived in the Dorset holiday town the year before, an unofficial evacuee from the East End of London. While Jack and his mother had been squeezing their own young evacuees into the damp, cramped rooms at Goonamarris, Ruth and her mother were settling into a roomy suburban house and the rhythms of a new life by the sea with a family called Wilkins.

They had come from Plaistow in East London, where Mabel and William Peaty had lived since before Ruth was born. Mabel's family hailed originally from Norwich, but they had moved to London when her father, Arnold Thomas, found work there as a signalman on the railways. Grandad Thomas, as Ruth called him, was a big-hearted man, always fond of a joke, who worked hard and liked nothing better than a pint or two at the local pub. His grandchildren could always wind him round their little fingers, and the highlight of their week was his regular Thursday visit to their home bearing a large bag of sweets. His wife, Alice, carried herself with more of an air. Her family had been in business in Norwich—their line was antiques—and she always seemed to her grandchildren to consider herself a cut or two above her husband. They had had three children: Eddie, who died from diphtheria at the age of seven; Frank, a harum-scarum dare-devil of a character who was forever playing pranks and getting into trouble; and Ruth's mother, Mabel Alice. She was a quieter child, teased mercilessly by Frank when they were young, with an intense side to her nature which was fed by a religious conversion at the age of thirteen at the Assembly Hall in East Ham. She was baptized there and attended regularly.

It was there that Mabel had met her first husband, Herbert Rhodes, a young gas-meter collector who approached her one day on a horse-drawn Sunday School outing and presented her with a mother-of-pearl brooch bearing her name. Their courtship proceeded quickly, hastened on by the outbreak of the First World War. Herbert's father had thought him too young to marry at twenty-two, for the money he was earning was desperately needed in the large Rhodes household, but Herbert was determined to claim his bride before he was sent to the Front.

Mabel and Herbert Rhodes were married in September 1915 and had one night together before his leave was over. Herbert had joined the Medical Corps so as not to be involved with the fighting. He was able to make one or two visits home to his new wife before leaving for the battlefield, but not many. Soon after he had gone, Mabel, like Eveline Clemo and thousands of other brides across the country, received a telegram informing her that her husband was dead. He had been killed in Flanders, blown up while carrying a Red Cross stretcher.

Heartbroken, Mabel went back to live with her mother and returned to her job in a draper's shop. She continued to attend the Assembly Hall and to teach her Sunday School class, but another plan was already forming in her mind. She would devote herself to missionary work, take herself off to India to work among the orphan children there. To this end she took a course in pharmacy, which would give her a useful skill in India, and finished off her last-minute preparations, ready to leave England for a long, long time. All that remained was the formality of going before the trustees of the Brethren Assembly to be passed as suitable for the job, and she would be off.

But at the last minute Mabel went down with tonsillitis. She was not to know how important her inflamed throat would one day prove in helping to fulfil the adult destiny of a baby then living many miles away in a tiny cottage in Cornwall. But she did soon realize how fateful a development it was to be in her own life, because in the time it took for her to recover from tonsillitis and for the trustees to arrange another session, she had met William Cecil Peaty.

William came from Poole in Dorset. His family had moved to London during his childhood. His father, William Peaty senior, was a builder's 'hodman' by trade, responsible for carrying bricks in an open trough, or hod, on the building site. He had never had much of an education, but he was a deeply religious man, famous for the extremely long prayers he came out with at Brethren meetings. Later on, in Ruth Peaty's own childhood, she always resigned herself to a cold dinner when Grandad Peaty was in charge of the Grace. She always thought of his wife, Arabella, as a rather refined lady, a bit like Grandma Thomas. Nana Peaty was an educated woman who shared her husband's religious convictions. They brought up their children, William and his sister Mabel, in the same faith.

In 1911, at the age of eighteen, William joined the Royal Marine Light Infantry. When war was declared in 1914 he was soon in active service. But although he survived the fighting, it was at tragic cost. He was a sensitive man, and like so many young soldiers and sailors in that dreadful war, his experience of combat and watching his comrades die blighted the rest of his life. The horrors he witnessed at the Battle of Jutland in May 1916 so turned his mind that he had to be invalided out of the Navy. His nerves were shattered and he was never the same again. His children would never forget the bald patch on the back of his head where no hair ever grew, or his explanation: 'It was the shock.'

Mabel Alice Rhodes met William Peaty at the Assembly Hall Bible Class. What she noticed first was the way the other girls were eyeing the new boy up. He was a good-looking young man with dark hair, a pale face and just that hint of a twinkle in the eye that always rouses interest in the female camp. Just to be different, Mabel made a point of not paying him any attention at all. But her determination began to waver when he started passing notes to her across the hall, intimating that despite her best efforts he had been smitten at first sight and she was The One for him.

Mabel did not make her mind up so quickly. She was convinced that what she had felt for Herbert Rhodes could never be repeated, and the pain at losing him was still acute. She also realized before long that William was ill. He was on sick leave from the Navy at the time, and his experiences of battle were still red and raw in his memory. There were signs already of the nervous trouble that would plague him for the rest of his life. And besides, Mabel reminded herself, she was going to India as a missionary.

In the end, however, she decided that marrying a sick young man who loved and needed her could in itself be a divine calling, as worthy a form of service as she would find anywhere on the other side of the world. They married quietly in a Registry Office in November 1919, two months after William's discharge from the Navy. In later years Mabel would advise her daughter gently to think carefully before embarking on a vocational marriage to a man with infirmities. For all the commitment and the mutual devotion, she came to know all too well how hard it could be in practice.

They set up home in a rented end terrace house in Edinburgh Road in the Plaistow area of East London. The house at the end of the row was a good one to get as you had a back door as well as a front door opening out on to the road. All their five children were born there.

Ruth Grace Peaty arrived on the scene in 1923. She was William and Mabel's second child. Their first-born, a fair-haired boy called John, died of a growth on his kidney at the age of two-and-a-half, only three months after the birth of his sister. Mabel was distraught. Although she lavished all her love on the new baby, she found—just as Eveline Clemo had—that losing her first child was an agony which would take a long time to ease.

Just under two years after Ruth was born, baby Arabella came along. This was one of the family's happiest periods. Mabel was content with her babies and William, whose health had improved

54

after his marriage, had a steady job as a 'relieving officer', monitoring financial assistance to the needy. He had been given the job of another man who, as late as 1921, had not yet returned from military service. William loved the work and, when there continued to be no sign of this man, came to feel that he had a secure job for life. He brought in enough money to provide Ruth and Bella with toys and to put up a summer house in the garden. On Sundays William was a lay preacher. Life was going well.

But then everything changed. The man whose job William had been given returned in 1927 to claim his place, and William found himself suddenly and unceremoniously out of work. It was a crushing blow. His health collapsed under the strain of not being able to support his family, and the nervous illness he had been more or less successfully fighting off returned. He spent years hunting for work, but jobs were hard to come by, and although he wrote off to every employer he could think of, it was without success. Ruth still has a copy of one note, written in the neat, sloping handwriting of the time and edged with despair:

> 20, Edinburgh Road,
> Plaistow E 13.
> 9/12/29
>
> Mr W. C. Peaty. Offers his services. 8 yrs RMLI. VG character. Worked for West Ham Guardians 1921–1927. Good references. Md. 3 children and wife. Badly needs regular and permanent work. Good book work. Clerk. Applies to you known as a Christian by Mr Burchill Forest Gate and Mr Elphick. Can you help?
>
> Yours Obediently
> W. C. Peaty

That employer could not help, nor would any other, and William never found another job. It hurt him keenly to have to queue to collect his dole money at the very office where he had once handed it out to others.

The family's difficulties had been intensified by the birth of another baby in 1927, just at the time William lost his job. The strain of coping with an ill husband, three children under five and all the financial worries was too much for Mabel Peaty and she was taken into hospital suffering from a nervous breakdown. While she recovered, Ruth and Bella were sent to an orphanage. The new-born baby, James, died soon afterwards.

Bella was too young to suffer much, but to this day Ruth remembers that time in the orphanage with horror. Jack had known the terrors of blindness at the age of five; now, at almost the same age, Ruth suddenly lost her mother and found herself in a strange, cold institution where she could neither eat nor sleep and lived in daily fear of the older, rougher children. Bewildered and ill, she pined for her mother and imagined that she was never going to get out, never ever.

She did get out, some months later, when Mabel was well enough to care for her daughters again. Ruth came home with rickets and a terrifying sense of insecurity that remained with her for years. Her mother did her best to restore her confidence, nursing her gently, assuring her that she was loved and would never be left again.

For all the difficulties of bringing her children up and all the suffering she endured over the years, Mabel Peaty was always a loving mother. It is a tribute to her resilience and to the Christian faith to which she held on through thick and thin, that after this painful period she was able to build a home that Ruth remembers as full of laughter. Mabel's breeziness rarely deserted her for long, and almost to the end of her life she managed to radiate fun. She had a perky, irrepressible sense of humour that her daughter inherited. As Ruth says, 'We needed it'—for there was more sorrow to come to the family.

Another baby, Jack, was born in 1929, the third child that William described in his job-application that December. But when the baby was only eighteen months old, William Peaty's nervous illness developed to a stage that required him to be taken permanently into hospital. He died there six years later, in January 1937, at the age of only forty-four.

Mabel struggled on alone with the three children, bringing them up in the Brethren fellowship where she and William had met. Ruth recalls pledging a personal faith there herself at the age of eleven. By that time she had developed into a lively child, still shy and a little reserved but something of a tomboy who liked nothing better than climbing the trees in Epping Forest with her sister and brother in tow. She had an inquisitive mind but little interest in formal schooling. Bella was the more studious of the two and continued her schooling as long as she could, but Ruth left school at fourteen. She simply thought it was the thing to do, and she knew her mother would be glad of the extra money. Mabel was bringing them up on her widow's pension and a meagre children's allowance. Ruth remembers being asked whether she wanted butter on her bread or margarine and jam; her mother could not afford both butter and jam. Ruth and Bella also had to learn the delicate art of halving a soft-boiled egg.

Ruth's first job was in a grocer's shop. She hated it and stayed only two weeks. Then she moved to a Jewish-owned ladies' lingerie factory, where she learned to be a machinist. There she enjoyed not only the work but all the additional Jewish holidays. In 1939 she was happily machining there when the outbreak of the Second World War heralded the collapse of the family's little world in Edinburgh Road. By the autumn of 1940, the Peatys had moved to Weymouth.

Evacuations from London were under way in the very first days of the war. In the uneasy weeks before the German invasion of Poland, the Government had asked local authorities all round the country to assess how many homes they could find for children from the large towns and cities most at risk from enemy attack. In Weymouth, then as now a thriving seaside town on the Dorset coast, the Mayor sent every householder a letter explaining the evacuation system. They would be paid 10s 6d a week for the first child billeted, and 8s 6d a week for every child after that. Even before war was declared, the first young evacuees had arrived, marching tearfully out of the station to the reception centres from which they were sent to their various billets. It was a traumatic time for children separated from their parents, finding themselves suddenly in a strange town with a strange family for whom the adjustment was likely to be proving equally difficult.

Compared to those children, the Peaty youngsters were lucky. They were not conventional evacuees. At the start of the war, Bella had been sent to Weymouth with her school and was put up there by a motherly lady called Mrs Wilkins. When Bella returned to London, Mrs Wilkins began to worry about her safety and that of her family. News was reaching Weymouth of blitzed houses and civilian deaths from air-raids on the capital. On 9 September 1940, she wrote to Mrs Peaty:

> I do hope that you are all three safe and well and that your home is still standing. It seems such a pity that after being in Weymouth all those months, Bella should return to London just in time to get in for the worst. I don't know how you are situated, but we wondered if we could come to your help by offering you and the two girls hospitality in our home for a while until things are quieter.

That letter changed the course of Ruth's life. The raids in London's East End were at their peak and she had not had a night's sleep for weeks. She was exhausted. Her factory was about to close down through lack of orders, so there was no problem about leaving her job. Since the youngest member of the family, eleven-year-old Jack, had already been evacuated to Wales with his school, that left the way clear. Mrs Peaty did not take long in accepting Mrs Wilkins' offer.

That autumn they packed up and left the children's lifetime home at 20 Edinburgh Road. The packing was not particularly thorough—this, after all, was supposed to be a temporary break from London 'until things were quieter'. As they locked the door and set off for the station, none of them dreamed for a moment that they would never be back. Their train fares were paid by the evacuation programme and later that day Mrs Wilkins, who received the standard remuneration for evacuees in return for her hospitality, welcomed them to a large house with a basement in the Rodwell suburb of Weymouth, overlooking Portland Harbour.

At first sight Weymouth scarcely looked like the haven they had been expecting. Thousands of sand-bags filled by volunteers had been placed around the town as a protection against bomb blast. The street lights were off, car headlights had been fitted with masks and the hotels were dark and silent. There were reports of drownings in the harbour as people lost their sense of direction along the blacked-out front. Sometimes you could hear the thunder of explosions out at sea when friendly steamers ran into German mines. Weymouth folk became used to the sight of strangers in their streets: shipwrecked sailors, French troops being withdrawn from Flanders, British people fleeing their homes when the enemy occupied the Channel Islands, and later Allied invasion troops, American GIs, and Italian prisoners passing through with their neatly combed black hair and frightened faces.

It was not long before Ruth realized that Weymouth was indeed going to prove no soft option to London. The town took a heavy hammering from enemy bombs and evacuations there were soon stopped. Once, a bomb fell only four doors away from their home, and Ruth couldn't help reflecting that while she had seen the dead and dying being pulled from houses and gardens further down their old road in Plaistow, they had never actually had a bomb drop quite as close as it had in Weymouth. On the other hand, the Weymouth bombing was not as relentless as it had been in London, night after night without respite. Grandad Thomas sent them reports of the obliteration of whole streets in Stratford where he lived. The old man had to move out at last to Southend, where he joined Grandma Thomas and effected a marital reunion. The two had been apart for years, but Hitler's bombs brought them together again at the close of their lives.

Ruth was happy in Weymouth. Despite the bombings and the streets packed with convoys of soldiers and the fortress mentality that began to grip the town as fears of a German invasion grew, she loved the 'feel' of the place from the first. She revelled in its closeness to the sea. She enjoyed the incongruous sight of palm trees along the parade, carelessly flaunting the evidence of Weymouth's mild climate.

Soon after she arrived, Bella and the younger of the two Wilkins girls said they had a surprise for her. They led her down to the Sandsfoot Castle Gardens not far from the house and ordered her to take a look. They knew how she would drink in the scene after the urban greyness of Plaistow, where you had to take a tram to reach a bit of greenery and a train to Southend to catch sight of the sea.

Here was an enchanted garden on her own doorstep, planted around the ruins of a castle built in the reign of Henry VIII after his break from the Roman Catholic Church. It was one of a series of fortifications that the king had ordered to be built along the south coast as a defence against any attempted invasion by the Pope's armies. Little remained of it now, but it was a lovely place to sit and contemplate the sea and bask among the rows of flowers, especially the roses in summer and the exotic flourish of palms. Ruth especially loved to watch the sea, stretching away for miles in front of her, ships ploughing their indolent course across the horizon and gulls crying above. Sandsfoot Castle Gardens became her favourite place in all the world, a haven to which she would bring all her doubts and heartbreaks in years to come, lolling on the grass here beside the remains of Henry's ancient castle and watching the sea-spray rise.

The family settled so smoothly into Weymouth life that it gradually dawned on them that no one felt much like going back to London. All three had managed to find jobs: Ruth in the Westham Laundry in Abbotsbury Road, Bella as a clerk in a building firm, and Mrs Peaty—venturing out to work for the first time since her marriage—in a draper's shop where the assistant had been called up. They had made a number of friends in the town, especially at the Open Brethren Assembly where they worshipped and where Ruth was baptized when she was eighteen. Young Jack Peaty was still at school in Wales, but by the time he was allowed to rejoin his family at the end of the war, Weymouth had become their permanent home.

Once they had finally decided not to return to London, the Peatys left the Wilkins' house and moved into a succession of furnished homes vacated by people who had departed hurriedly when the bombing started. They found a suitable empty house for rent in 1941 and sent for their own furniture from London. As there were no removal vans available during the war, the furniture had to make the journey in an open railway truck and most of it was damaged on the way. But it was good to see the familiar old tables and chairs again, and the family were soon comfortably settled in the new house, 24 Southlands Road, Rodwell, just up the road from Ruth's beloved castle gardens. It was an address that Jack Clemo would one day come to know very well indeed.

Ruth was delighted with her job as a packer in one of the town's main laundries. It was a reserved occupation. (She had considered the land army, but decided on reflection that she didn't like cows.) The laundry's task during the war was to keep the Forces in clean uniforms. Ruth's duty was 'packing and racking', sorting the linen out by numbers. She also had to darn socks—'those awful grey woolly socks', she recalls with a grimace—leaving her initials R.P. on the card that accompanied each batch. All the girls did that. If you were lucky you got a letter back beginning, 'Dear R.P.', or a bar of chocolate, or in the case of some of the girls, a spot of romance.

The laundry girls were never short of admirers. Weymouth was full of soldiers and sailors with time on their hands, and when the American GIs arrived on the scene in 1944 the pace of life hotted up considerably. The Americans started up dances, while the local bands struggled manfully to master the new-fangled rhythms of jive and boogie-woogie. There were baseball games to watch and a perceptible increase in the 'Dear R.P.' sort of letter in the laundry post. Ruth enjoyed the lively atmosphere of the town, but she never went to any of the dances and didn't feel it was quite the proper thing to mix with the GIs. She felt sorry for some of them, though: the lonely-looking ones who came into the laundry and said they were off the next day and did not know whether they would live or die.

That summer she joined most of the population of Weymouth out on the streets to watch, heart in mouth, as the troops left for the D-Day invasion of Normandy—great long convoys of lorries and tanks filled with boyish American soldiers in their green uniforms, cracking jokes and winking at the girls as they moved across the harbour in their hundreds. It made Ruth sad to think of what awaited these and the other soldiers she had known when they reached the opposite shores. The least she could do, she reckoned, was to write to as many as had left their names.

Ruth was a compulsive letter-writer, and she liked to think that she could bring some cheer to a soldier at the Front by passing on little items of news and reminding him of a verse or two of Scripture that she hoped would give comfort when times were bad. One correspondent began to interest her particularly. He was a young British marine whom she had never met but who had been given her name as someone who might prove a sympathetic pen-friend. He was serving at sea and was a member of the Royal Marine Band. The marine's first letter started off with a quotation from a poem, which intrigued Ruth immediately. She liked poetry. Subsequent letters revealed that he belonged, like her, to the Brethren fellowship and was extremely lonely. Ruth wrote back enthusiastically, addressing her letters care of the GPO in London, from where they were sent on to his ship.

Before long this relationship was absorbing her whole attention and other, more altruistic correspondence dropped off. They wrote regularly for two years, quoting the Bible—their chief mutual interest—happily to one another, indulging in what Ruth called 'Bible study by mail', and gradually revealing more and more about themselves as the correspondence progressed. Not surprisingly, a certain warmth crept into their letters after a while and they longed for the end of the war so that they could meet and find out how serious their feelings really were.

When the war was finally over, the marine returned to his home at Plymouth and began to visit Ruth at weekends in Weymouth, a Weymouth that was gradually returning to Punch and Judy shows on the beach and ice-creams on the esplanade. The two were deeply attracted to one another. Ruth had had plenty of casual boyfriends, but never had she experienced an emotion as strong or intense as this. She was wholly and ecstatically in love.

She spent the Christmas of 1946 with his family in Plymouth, and it was there that she and her young marine (whose name she prefers, even today, not to disclose) decided to get married the following year. Post-war conditions meant she had to do without an engagement ring, but Ruth returned to Weymouth in the New Year utterly contented. She waited eagerly for the promised bliss to materialize.

6

Christ in the Clay-Pit

While Ruth was dreaming of weddings in Weymouth, there was excitement of a different kind at Goonamarris. Great things were happening on the literary front at the beginning of 1947. After more than fifteen years and fifty-three rejection slips, Jack had at long last had a novel accepted by a publisher.

The jubilation in the household was heady. This was not just a breakthrough, a dream come true, a mountain scaled. To Jack and his mother the acceptance of *Wilding Graft* was nothing less than a miracle. It had taken five years to get this far with the book. Jack had begun writing in February 1942, fresh from reading Thomas Hardy's *Tess of the d'Urbervilles* and *Jude the Obscure* (bought with a book-token won in a Methodist Guild essay competition) and then, with mounting excitement, Hardy's other classic, *The Return of the Native*. He found Hardy's lyrically brooding fatalism instantly attractive, his style an ideal vehicle for the 'poetic Calvinism' Jack was setting out to incorporate into his own novel.

The words came easily. Jack wrote steadily at the rate of two chapters a month for fourteen months and closed his typewriter at last with satisfaction. He was sure that it was the best thing he had written to date. Into it he had poured his own hopes and convictions, his own theology as it had developed thus far, and above all his own dream of romantic fulfilment. Even today, the novel conveys a feeling of raw, exposed nerves.

The plot is simple. It is the story of a clay-labourer, Garth Joslin, and his love for a fifteen-year-old London girl called Irma. She is driven from him by the scandal-mongers of a village community who cannot understand the nature of his spiritually intense love. The core of the book is Garth's trial of faith as he waits for God to vindicate his conviction that they are 'meant' for one another; which God obligingly does before the last page. The character of Irma was drawn largely from that of the nine-year-old evacuee Irene, although the details of the love-affair were entirely imaginary. But Garth, the hero, is all Jack, or at least Jack as he liked to see himself at that time: a man buffeted by misfortune and loss, a man of apocalyptic prayer, stubborn hope, invincible faith. There is little irony in the book.

What Jack set out to do in the novel, as he explained later, was to demonstrate that God can '*create* a point of contact at any level of the human personality—not only in the so-called higher levels of idealism and spirituality, but in the undisciplined instinct, a direct grafting into the life-blood of passion instead of into the cool boney structure of reason.' It was the concept that he had been struggling to express since his teens—'Christ's own face can glow/In love's embrace, and kisses be as prayers'—and that had provided a channel to conversion in his twenties: the idea that a divine conquest of human nature can operate through the senses. In a way, *Wilding Graft* is Jack Clemo's first manifesto.

If the novel and the characterization suffer from being used so overtly as a vehicle for Jack's theology, it is not something for which he would apologize. As he was to write in the preface to *Confession of a Rebel*: 'I am one of those writers whose creative work cannot be fully understood without reference to certain broken boundaries in their private lives.'

Jack finished the novel in April 1943, but with the war still at its height he knew it would be crazy to try to get it published there and then. So he placed the manuscript carefully in a drawer in the dresser alongside the dozens of other manuscripts that had already travelled the road to London and back many times. Only in peacetime conditions, he reckoned, would such an idiosyncratic work as *Wilding Graft* stand a chance of rousing interest.

But peace was a long time in coming, or so it felt to Jack, confined to his cottage with nothing to do and the best novel he had ever written lying uselessly in a drawer. He tried to make a start on new projects, but to his horror discovered that his creative energy was flagging pitiably. He wondered if *Wilding Graft* had somehow burned him out, just as he was getting somewhere with his writing. The months dragged by, and all he was capable of doing was to revise work that had already been rejected. It took considerable effort just to make himself sit down at the typewriter and do that. He began to panic. By November 1943 he was writing in his diary:

> This idleness is pulling me to pieces, and the monotony gets more horrible every day . . . Day after day I spend hanging round the bookcase from morning to night, taking out book after book, dipping into it and putting it back—can't get interested. It's a travesty of life and gets me to hate reading and everything bookish, and that in turn paralyzes me as a writer. God restore the true fire of me, or I shall be, like poor Thompson, 'an icicle whose thawing is its dying'.

The monotony of life at this time was reinforced by his penury. He and his mother were so short of money that he could not think of taking a trip to the seaside or the cinema to relieve the dullness. Nor could he afford the postage on the uncommissioned freelance articles that had once occupied him; the chances of their being rejected were too high to justify even the investment of a few pence.

He was also missing adult company. The children were still around, and provided his only stimulation, but his deafness excluded him from the company of the old men in the district whose anecdotes he had loved as a boy. He could not even join in the conversations that his mother enjoyed at the garden gate, the trivia of community affairs, the latest rumours about the war. All his information was limited to information or questions passed on scraps of paper: 'One cake or two for tea, Jack?' 'Nothing in the post today.'

The war seemed to drag on interminably. Day after day Jack

read in his newspaper of the Japanese making further gains in the Far East, or the Nazis penetrating deeper into Russia. What hope for *Wilding Graft* now?

The Allies' own war effort had by this time arrived at his own front door, as Goonamarris was inside the military zone that now stretched across southern England in preparation for the Second Front in Europe. There were Canadian troops encamped on the downs at Rostowrack, American soldiers in rows of tents at Trethosa and Italian prisoners-of-war working at the various clayworks dotted around the neighbourhood. The narrow country roads were clogged with Army jeeps and there were American guards around every corner demanding permits and evidence of identity. Jack felt most uncomfortable passing these check-points; his deafness made it difficult for him to explain his business and he had the distinct impression that he was regarded as a suspicious character.

As D-Day approached, vehicles carrying camouflaged guns began to trundle through Goonamarris, bound for Normandy. While Ruth was out on the streets watching the convoys of troops moving slowly along Chesil Beach towards the waiting ships in Portland Harbour, Jack was gazing in awed fascination at another stream of lorries and field ambulances heading for the same battlefield as they jerked and jolted their way down the valley beyond his bedroom window.

Far from feeling immune to the war, as he had when it started, Jack was now nearly wild with the frustration of being unable to get to grips with all this drama unfolding around him. It ought to have been a writer's wonderland, and indeed his imagination was reeling with nightmare images of combat and destruction. But he couldn't *hear* what was going on. As he says: 'The whole district was teeming with stories I couldn't get at.' He was unable to pick up the anecdotes, the gossip, the telling incidents, the human colour that might have sparked off a new novel. He had no access to dialogue or to accent. He couldn't engage a soldier in conversation or find out how the troops were living and the locals responding.

The nearest he came to human contact was with the Italian prisoners who were employed on building projects down the road at Goonvean claywork. They were transported to and from the works every day, and while waiting for their buses would sit on the hedge opposite Jack's cottage and stare at him as he lounged at his desk. It was not long before Jack was at the receiving end of the Latin charm that had already bowled over half the female population of the district. One of the Italians asked Mrs Clemo if the young man at the desk were not perhaps a poet, as he had an artistic look about him. Before long they were crowding into the cottage to shake his hand, kneel at his desk and peruse his manuscripts. One sergeant informed Mrs Clemo decisively that 'Florence is the place for him'. Jack, who had never received the slightest attention from any of his own countrymen, could not help basking in the uninhibited flattery.

But for all the Italian praise, Jack was unhappily aware that his creativity was now at a standstill. As the Allies continued their push across Europe, he spent much of his time wandering among the clayfields that the troops had vacated, self-consciously shunning the villages where he imagined people pointing him out pityingly to one another as the young man whose early promise had come to nothing.

Then in February 1945, quite without warning, he came in from a stroll round Goonvean claywork one Sunday afternoon, sat down at his desk and found himself writing this:

> Why should I find Him here
> And not in a church, nor yet
> Where Nature heaves a breast like Olivet
> Against the stars? I peer
> Upon His footsteps in this quarried mud;
> I see His blood
> In rusty stains on pit-props, waggon-frames
> Bristling with nails, not leaves. There were no leaves
> Upon His chosen Tree,

No parasitic flowering over shames
Of Eden's primal infidelity.

They are the opening lines of 'Christ in the Clay-Pit', lines, he says, 'which I knew at once were the finest poetry I had ever penned'. With that poem Jack Clemo found his poetic voice, the medium in which he would from now on communicate his most deep-felt insights. Barred by deafness from writing any more novels, he would turn increasingly after this to poetry as the vehicle of his visions. It was a faculty he thought had gone for ever with the immature fancies of the Evelyn years; now it returned, uninvited and unannounced, to serve him when his creativity was at its most parched.

Jack's spirits lifted further as it became obvious that the end of the war was in sight. His thoughts returned to the novel in the drawer, and at long last he felt confident enough to despatch it to his recently acquired literary agent, Raymond Savage. That summer it fell to Mr Savage to hawk the precious *Wilding Graft* manuscript round the publishers of the bomb-blasted capital. With the troops pouring back, stories of valour on all sides, the streets ringing with victory celebrations, it was not easy to interest anyone in a novel set in war-time but which scarcely mentioned the war, a novel whose characters lived in an obscure industrial corner of Cornwall and whose hero kept talking rather personally about God. The manuscript returned to Mr Savage's desk with unflagging regularity.

At Goonamarris Jack awaited the postman's call every day with painful excitement. He was still waiting, sick with disappointment as the weeks passed in silence, when the last shaft of brightness in his domestic life disappeared. The evacuees went home.

He had dreaded this moment as 'an expulsion from the last of my "little Edens", with nothing but a grey inhuman wilderness beyond', although in more optimistic moods he had allowed himself to hope that the end of his 'child-friendships' might usher in the real love of which he dreamed. In the event, the departure of Irene and the other children whom Goonamarris had acquired over the war years passed off without drama. It provoked none of the violent grief he had felt at the loss of Barbara all those years ago. The children's going simply left his life a little more bleak and his home a great deal more empty than before.

It was the hopes for his novel, still bravely doing the rounds of the London publishing houses, that kept Jack going. But in November and then December 1945 Mr Savage reported failure. Publishers whom he had thought might be interested had proved not to be. It was a gloomy Christmas that year, heavy with the feeling of failure. The strain produced a brief attack of eye-trouble and Jack spent most of the festive season in semi-blindness. The following February came news of another rejection. Reluctantly Jack made some revisions that Mr Savage thought might improve its chances.

In August his hopes soared with the news that one publisher had at last expressed an interest. There was only one objection in the way—the ending would have to be made 'less feeble'. Obediently Jack rewrote the closing chapters and sent the manuscript back. The publisher turned it down.

But the end was now in sight. That publisher softened his rejection (the seventh that *Wilding Graft* had collected) by suggesting that Chatto and Windus might be interested; and sure enough, within two weeks of seeing it, they made an offer. Jack's manifesto, his great literary treasure, was on the way to publication at last.

It is hard to say who was the more delighted—Jack or his mother. Mrs Clemo felt that the promise received so long ago had been kept. For so many years she had shared with Jack the pain of literary rejection, struggled to follow his mind along the strange paths he roamed and worried desperately about where it would all end. Now she believed that Jack's success with an overtly religious novel had vindicated her trust that her child would be 'taught of the Lord'.

It was in 1948, almost two years later, that *Wilding Graft* was actually published. Critical reaction was generally positive, and the novel won Jack an Atlantic Award in Literature worth £100 from Birmingham University. It was published in America and translated into Swedish. The *New York Times* praised the Hardyesque touch in his evocation of the clayscape and noted a nineteenth-century flavour which gave the book 'a certain stature seldom seen in distinctly modern fiction'. Another critic, Walter Allen, dismissed it politely with the words: 'The novel, I think, fails.'

But a fulsome tribute was paid by the Cornish writer and critic A. L. Rowse, whose review is reprinted in part on the cover of the 1983 Anthony Mott edition of *Wilding Graft*. 'This novel has haunted my mind for days,' he wrote. '. . . Out of the harsh realism, true to the country and the people he comes from, the singular intenseness and vivacity of the Cornish temperament, he has wrung a strange beauty. He is of the spiritual progeny of that greatest of West Country writers, Thomas Hardy.'

It was a proud moment for Jack when he saw his novel on the bookstands for the first time. His pleasure was clouded only by the thought, nagging uncomfortably at the back of his mind, that the happy ending trumpeted in a book so blatantly autobiographical in other ways had not yet come about in his own life. He had written *Wilding Graft* as an act of faith, believing that the consecrated love that had come to his hero after years of waiting would come also to him. But where was she?

It was Jack's mother who put her finger on what was troubling him in the midst of his triumph. 'Your own Irma 'aven't come,' she remarked. 'It *do* spoil it.'

In the two years between the acceptance of the novel and its publication Jack had been writing poetry. The poem which had 'come upon him' so unexpectedly just before the end of the war pointed towards the future. It was the earliest expression of what was to become a familiar Clemo idiom, the first of a series of poems—composed sporadically over the next few years—in which he exploited all the symbolic potential of the landscape in which he had grown up to express the faith he lived by and the

71

love he longed for.

At their best these early clay-poems have a disturbing power. In 'The Excavator', for instance, he prays:

> Keep far from me all loveliness, O God,
> And let me laud
> Thy meaner moods, so long unprized:
> The motions of that twisted, dark,
> Deliberate crucial Will
> I feel deep-grinding still
> Under the dripping clay with which I am baptized.

Jack's image of the cross in this poem is startlingly original: it is the interlinking bars of the mechanical digger which, he says, may lack the symmetry of the crosses you find in churches,

> . . . but is more
> Like His whose stooping tore
> The vitals from our world's foul secrecy.
> This too has power to worm
> The entrails from a flint, bearing the scoop
> With every searching swoop—
> That broken-mouthed gargoyle
> Whose iron jaws bite the soil,
> Snapping with sadist kisses in the soft
> White breasts of rocks, and ripping the sleek belly
> Of sprawling clay-mounds, lifting as pounded jelly
> Flower roots and bush tufts with the reeking sand.

It is not very comfortable poetry, but Jack's aim was to express what he considered to be some of the less comfortable aspects of God's sovereignty over human life, in reaction to what he called 'the pagan slop of nature poets'. To Jack, the 'upheaval' on his door step represented 'tough truth attacking sentimental falsehood', and there is an element of crusading zeal in the poems of this period.

When they were later published together in his first collection, *The Clay Verge*, many critics were repelled. It seemed to some reviewers to be a grim, ugly sort of religion that Jack was upholding in such vicious images, although there was a fairly consistent respect for the vigour and the sincerity with which it was expressed. In fact, Jack himself came to realize in time that the stark claywork symbolism was to some extent giving vent to a distorted vision. Lines like these, in 'The Clay-Tip Worker', are very much the product of private unresolved tensions:

> I love to see the sand and stone I tip
> Muzzle the grass and burst the daisy heads;
> I watch the hard waves lapping out to still
> The soil's rhythm for ever, and I thrill
> With solitary song upon my lip,
> Rejoicing as the refuse spreads:
> 'Praise God, the earth is maimed,
> And there will be no daisies in that field
> Next spring; it will not yield
> A single bloom or grass blade: I shall see
> In symbol potently
> Christ's Kingdom there restored:
> One patch of Poetry reclaimed
> By Dogma: one more triumph for our Lord.'

Even Jack's mother thought he was going a bit far with that one. In verse like that, unmatched in poetic intensity by anything he wrote later in more balanced mood, Jack was speaking out of his own fierce loneliness. The destructive images of war were still strongly in his imagination and the frustrations of those empty years still tearing at his heart. His Christianity was a stark faith at the time, worked out in the vacuum of his clay wilderness, not yet humanized by fellowship. He was still angrily alienated from the churches and anything that smacked of 'easy' religion or 'God-in-a-flower' sentimentality.

This was the poetry of Jack Clemo's unhappy days. Perhaps

that is ultimately the source of power in the clay poems, which, as they came to be published in different collections over the years, earned him a reputation as an iron visionary—'about as easily digested as hot steel ingots,' said the journalist Kenneth Allsop in 1961. It is also perhaps why in more recent years Jack has sought to distance himself from it, arguing that the more mellow verse of his maturity represents his true, undistorted vision.

Nevertheless, the poems that spurted from him in the late nineteen-forties remain among his finest. At a time when his own inner life was scarred and bleak, the images of a scarred landscape rushed spontaneously from his pen. The vision was incomplete and harsh, but he had found a medium for presenting it brilliantly.

The next chapter of his life would introduce him to other dimensions of the truth. Up till now his faith had taught him to surrender, but not yet to sing. He knew a lot in theory about divine grace, but not so much about divine graciousness. His poems celebrated the uncomfortable aspects of the Christian revelation, positively exulting in the idea of the Excavator-God; he had not yet learned to dance to the beat of what he would later call 'God's jazz'. Nor had he yet come into contact with the people—and one woman in particular—who could teach him that there was peace and beauty in the world after all, if he only knew how to look.

On Palm Sunday 1947, Jack awoke with another of the semiblind attacks which had struck him intermittently since childhood. His right eye was inflamed, his left eye weak and his sight blurred. He was taken immediately to hospital in St Austell, where he spent ten days in bed being regularly injected with penicillin. He lay there waiting as patiently as he could—'After all, this was Passion Week, and I was supposed to be a mystic' — for the treatment to take effect.

On a small table by his bed there was a copy of *Penguin New Writing* in which some of his recent poems had been included. One of these was 'A Calvinist in Love', which Jack later described as an attempt at his own brand of the Browning love-poem. It begins:

> I will not kiss you, country fashion,
> > By hedgesides where
> > Weasel and hare
> Claim kinship with our passion,
>
> I care no more for fickle moonlight:
> > Would rather see
> > Your face touch me
> Under a claywork dune-light.
>
> I want no scent or softness round us
> > When we embrace:
> > We could not trace
> Therein what beauties bound us.
>
> This bare clay-pit is truest setting
> > For love like ours:
> > No bed of flowers
> But sand-ledge for our petting.

And it ends with a statement, inspired by Browning but pure Clemo in expression, of love as a Christian offering:

> Our love is full-grown Dogma's offspring,
> > Election's child,
> > Making the wild
> Heats of our blood an offering.

Jack records that as he lay alone in his hospital room, thinking of that verse, he wondered what sort of woman it would take to understand what on earth he was on about, and where she might be now.

7

Ruth in Training

No one has recorded exactly what Ruth Peaty was thinking that Palm Sunday in 1947 when Jack Clemo's thoughts were on 'A Calvinist in Love'. The chances are that she was dreaming of her marine, since that is what she did most days. He had been writing to her practically every day since their engagement at Christmas and they met up every weekend that he had off-duty. He was stationed near Plymouth, and he either travelled to Weymouth to see her or they met halfway in Exeter.

Plans for their wedding in August were proceeding happily. He intended to go back to sea for two-and-a-half years after they were married, and he had his eye on the house he wanted them to settle down in on his return. While he was away, Ruth would stay with her mother and sister, as she knew hardly anyone in Plymouth.

By July, Ruth had just about collected enough clothing coupons to buy herself a trousseau. She was at the stage of debating exactly what to take with her on honeymoon when a letter arrived. She opened it eagerly, sure that she knew what it would be about. Her fiancé had gone to Wales to arrange a week's stay there on the honeymoon, to follow the week they had already arranged to spend in Scotland. He had said he would write when it was all fixed.

But that letter contained very different news. It informed her that the wedding was off. He was sorry, but he just didn't feel 'right' about it all of a sudden . . . just one of those things. Ruth could hardly take in what the letter was saying. It was shattering enough to have her engagement broken off out of the blue, quite without warning; but even more so when she had invested such an intense religious emotion in it all. Immersed in their 'Bible study by mail' and then in heavy devotional sessions together, she had always assumed that this relationship of theirs must figure pretty solidly in the divine plan. *He* had certainly talked enough about it being 'God's will' for them to marry.

Now, apparently, it wasn't. When her marine came to see her after the letter, he said he couldn't explain what had changed. Nothing had happened, no one else was on the scene; the idea of marriage just felt wrong. Nevertheless Ruth did think she detected an element of hesitation. He didn't seem quite as sure as he had in his letter that they could *never* make a go of it. Perhaps, he hinted, this was to be a 'time of testing' for their relationship. Perhaps if they stayed apart for a while and devoted themselves to the things of God, it would all become clear in the future.

So Ruth had lost him, but not completely—which only intensified the hurt. At first she was numb with the pain of it. Then as time passed, she began to devote herself more and more to earnest religious contemplation. He had asked her to do that; he had said he would do the same thing. She decided she would wait for him like a nun, sublimating her feelings for him and concentrating on eternal things.

She took herself off whenever she could to her refuge, Sandsfoot Castle Gardens, aching for him to come back as she looked out on the vessels at sea and wondered where his ship was now, but trying as hard as she could to pray and study and keep her thoughts in spiritual channels. She says that amidst the pain she had many a joyous mystical moment there, 'communing with the eternal love'. It was all a deeply private experience, difficult to relate from the outside, impertinent to comment upon. But one day, over twenty years later, Jack Clemo would understand perfectly when Ruth told him about this bitter-sweet time in her life. And she, in turn, would have no difficulty in entering the world of his visionary imagination and identifying with those moments of heart-searing insight when he too had seen heaven and earth in a new way.

Ruth waited a long time for her marine: almost eight years. In the meantime, the rest of her life flowed along uneventfully. The biggest drama of those years came right at the beginning, at the same time as her engagement was breaking up. A huge fire at the Westham Steam Laundry that July made her think she was going to lose her job as well as her marriage. The ironing room was gutted and thousands of pounds worth of clothing and linen destroyed. But the laundry managed to stay open and Ruth was kept busy working extra shifts so that the hotels could be kept in clean bedding at the peak of their summer season.

Ruth continued to enjoy her work there, sorting out the items of clothing and packing them into parcels or hampers for delivery. She was at a table near the reception area where she could talk easily to the customers as they passed in and out, and she came to know several of them well. Sometimes one or other would slip her a little present if she had managed to put their laundry through quickly. A local butcher presented her graciously with a large pork chop one day for servicing his white overalls so speedily.

Weymouth in the late forties and early fifties was returning to the thriving holiday resort it had been before the war. Ruth lived a little way out from the centre, but she could tell how busy the tourist seasons had become again by the bulk of laundry she had to handle and the amount of overtime she and her workmates were asked to put in. Everyone seemed to be on holiday except them. When she strolled along the esplanade as she sometimes did on Sundays, the scene was of a typically English seaside: creamy sand, boiled bodies, stalls selling jellied eels, striped deckchairs, Punch and Judy, and a flag fluttering high over the beach announcing 'Lost Children'. It was fun to watch, but Ruth's own taste was for Weymouth's more hidden corners, like the castle gardens or the wind-whipping cliffs of Portland Bill.

She did little in those years except work, walk and study devotional books. It was a lonely time. She had renounced men and saw herself as a sort of Heloise figure keeping herself for her Abelard. She might have waited a lifetime, had it not been for a piece of news that filtered through to her from a friend in 1954. Her marine, whom she had only once seen but had never stopped thinking about since 1947, was married. He had tied the knot with a local Plymouth girl whom he had known all his life.

Ruth was devastated. Eight years of waiting—and all for this. All that earnest contemplation to attune herself with 'the will of God'—and this was how it ended. She was hurt and angry and utterly desolate. She railed at God, questioned her faith and looked back in disbelief at what she now saw as the naivety of her understanding in the years of waiting that had now ended so unceremoniously. It was undoubtedly a turning-point in her life. Although as time passed she would once again become what she calls 'alive to God and mystical', what she suffered in 1954 revolutionized her approach to religious matters. 'I had intellectual queries now,' she recalls, 'and I wondered how what I had always accepted blindly could be true.'

She began to read the sort of books she would never have gone near in the past: books by Jung, Kierkegaard, Aquinas; books about the unconscious mind, about pain and loss, God and suffering; books about love. She turned in particular to a volume called *Studies in Browning*, as 'he seemed to know what human love was all about'. But she found little peace. She was restless and confused, searching for answers without being entirely sure what the question was. She longed for contact with a mind that would help her towards a synthesis, someone with a Christian vision that could accommodate the realities of human pain and doubt.

If you had the task of devising a training course which would prepare a wife for Jack Clemo, you could try for a century without coming up with anything better than the one Ruth Peaty was going through. She knew what it was to be jilted, to wait and desire and hope without satisfaction. She knew all about the pain of loss. She understood loneliness. She also had a mystical bent when the mood was upon her, although even during her most ecstatic 'communings' in the castle gardens it appears that her feet were planted firmly on the flagstones. Her Christianity was the orthodox evangelicalism in which she had been educated since infancy, but she was beginning to apply her mind to it at last, to address herself to problems with which Jack also struggled.

And to round off the training, she was becoming fascinated by the relationship between human and divine love. Browning, she felt, might have the clue.

If anyone could take on a complicated character like Jack Clemo, with the mind of an artist, the soul of a preacher and the heart of a lover, it was surely Ruth Peaty. But there was a long way to go yet before either of them knew it.

8

Love's Labour's Lost

Jack was in love. Her name was Eileen, she was eighteen years old, and she had caught his imagination as early as 1946 with a particularly fervent article in a religious magazine. Three years later, while Ruth was deep in her Heloise phase, Jack spotted another article by the same author. Its tone of youthful enthusiasm for the earth's loveliness gave him a twinge of vague unease about some of his own more violently anti-nature poems and, intrigued to know more about the girl, he wrote her a letter, care of the magazine. She replied at once and there began a correspondence which lasted for several months.

Jack was, so to speak, on the look-out. Understandably so. A man who has not the slightest opportunity of meeting young women but who believes his destiny is to marry, will be more susceptible than most to encouraging letters from a girl who says she likes poetry. Eileen was the first woman with whom Jack, now in his thirties, had ever established what he felt to be a fairly normal relationship—even if it *was* at pen's length. She was a lonely, sensitive girl who wrote poems which Jack privately thought a bit sentimental. Their letters to one another were relaxed, honest and chatty, and in time Jack decided that things had progressed far enough for him to broach the delicate subject of Wimpole Street and his belief in a divine vocation for marriage.

When Eileen inquired doubtfully how he could be so sure that marriage was his destiny, he promptly posted off to her a copy of a poem of his that had just been published in the *Cornish Review*, called 'Intimate Landscape'. This, he fancied, ought to prove beyond doubt that he was not just fantasizing about love but that, although without experience, he really did have an insight into marital sensitivities:

Oh darling, lead me safely through the world:
Make clear each sign lest my male clay be hurled
To flame when it seeks cooling, or to ice
When lava leaps in you, hot veins entice
Beneath a white breast I misread,
Thinking it cold, and pass unconscious of your need.

Eileen appeared to be suitably impressed. But there was still one small problem. They had exchanged photographs, and, not to put too fine a point on it, she didn't much fancy the look of him. Jack had to admit that her looks didn't do much for him either, but, never a man to give up easily, he tried another tack. Might not the senses be enjoyed 'sacramentally' rather than biologically? he hazarded. Eileen remained doubtful.

Gradually her letters began to reflect another worry—her growing unease about his handicaps. Eileen's parents had been impressing upon her the difficulties that would be involved in marriage to a deaf man, and eventually she acted. Jack was appalled to receive a letter one day containing an ultimatum. Unless he were miraculously healed within one month, wrote Eileen, she would take it as a sign that their friendship should go no further. Jack accepted with glum resignation; he had little choice. In fact, the letter breaking off their relationship arrived some days before the expiry of the miracle deadline.

He was not greatly surprised in the end. But the rejection hurt all the same; it hurt very much. For eight months he had immersed himself with all-consuming dedication in the first semblance of adult romance he had known, and the days that followed the cessation of that precious friendship were empty ones indeed.

As time passed, however, Jack was able to detect lasting benefits from knowing Eileen. He wrote later: 'The soft sway of a young feminine personality, which shared my faith but was free from my distortions, had begun to clear away the effects of deep emotional wounding. Of all the people I then knew, she was the only one who could have done it. My mother had always found me stubborn. I would not listen to her when she told me to go to chapel, or get a job, or "look a bit more tidy". I hadn't listened to her when she said that my readers would think me a crank if I wrote religious denunciations of flowers. My quirks had sprung from lack of a mature girl's tenderness and understanding. Eileen had given me these qualities.'

While Jack's romantic hopes waned, there was at least the taste of success in his literary life. In 1949 *Confession of a Rebel*, an autobiography undertaken at the request of the publishers of his novel, was published. It is a remarkable document, the story of Jack's life as far as the acceptance of *Wilding Graft* when he was thirty, eloquently written and achingly honest. Jack writes without much pretence at ironical detachment from the processes of his own inner life, and that can at times be wearing; but the sheer intensity with which he experiences life and relates that experience is compelling.

The central thesis of the book is summed up towards the end, where he writes: '. . . I had paid a heavy price—a price that made my hair turn grey before I was twenty-eight—to prove what I had set out to prove: that creeds rejected by most of my contemporaries as dead superstition could still enable a man to find his place in the world, despite the most grievous handicaps, and that the claim of the schools to be indispensable to intellectual development, and to success in literature, is nonsense.'

The Sunday Times hailed *Confession of a Rebel* as a 'classic of autobiography' and the *New Statesman* called it 'a rugged and naive book, sincere, moving and frank'. Even while disagreeing, sometimes rather forcibly, with the views expressed in it, reviewers paid extravagant tribute to its originality and its compulsive frankness. 'A work of genius', raved *Country Life* magazine. *The Listener* described it as 'a remarkable and extraordinary book'.

At Goonamarris the composition of the Clemo household had changed again. In the summer of 1948 two foster-children joined the family. Mrs Clemo was missing the noise and laughter that the London evacuees had brought to the house during the war

83

and was keen to try a more permanent fostering arrangement. Violet and Frances Allen, aged twelve and eleven, arrived one day in the company of a female welfare officer from Plymouth and settled in with remarkably little fuss. They came from a broken family and had spent much of their lives in a children's home, but they were soon devoted to Mrs Clemo. Jack grew fond of both his new sisters, whose company enlivened the home without influencing his artistic creativity one way or another. That phase was now over.

The other change was a sad one. In March 1949 little Aunt Bertha took ill and died. Throughout the whole of Jack's life she had been a constant presence in the cottage, shrivelled and stunted from her premature birth, never participating much in the family dramas but always cheerful, always laughing. Jack would remember with affection her familiar screech—'Lor' massy'—that had rung round the house from his earliest years. Bertha left a bigger hole in the household than her diminutive frame had ever occupied.

Financially, it was still a struggle for the family. Jack's royalties were small and *Confession of a Rebel*, for all its critical acclaim, did not bring in much money. It was at this time that two eminent literary figures took up Jack's cause. They were the poet C. Day Lewis, who had read and enjoyed the clay poems, and the critic A. L. Rowse, who had been so impressed by *Wilding Graft*. Both men offered Jack help and encouragement in his writing, but they were also of more practical assistance in sponsoring an appeal to the Royal Literary Fund, which awarded Jack a grant. This eased the family's economic difficulties for the time being and gave Jack a new sense of security as a writer.

He also received help of a different kind from a Somerset author called Monica Hutchings, who was responsible for arranging a momentous event in his life in the summer of 1950. A three-day trip to Dorset might not seem momentous to anyone else, but to Jack, who rarely travelled anywhere and was extraordinarily sensitive to the spirit of a place, it was of enormous significance. Monica had read *Confession of a Rebel* and been struck by the admiration Jack often expressed there for the Dorset mystical writer, T. F. Powys. She offered to take Jack and his mother to meet the old seer and Jack, mindful that Dorset was also Thomas Hardy country, accepted at once. (It was Ruth Peaty country as well, had he only known it, and during that trip he passed within a few dozen miles of her, still working in the Weymouth laundry and waiting for her marine.)

Powys was a big, sturdy, white-haired old man who welcomed them warmly to his home at Mappowder. Jack was sorry not to be able to join in the animated conversation that carried on around him. How he would have loved to talk to this man whose writing had been such an influence on his own work. But Jack loved the homely, book-laden atmosphere and drank in the whole experience to mull over later at home.

That Dorset visit proved to be something of a watershed in his life. Jack left the Powys home in the balmy sunshine of a late summer afternoon, suffused with a deep contentment. As he wrote later: 'My faith, including my confidence about my marriage, was strangely quickened, fused with the warm mellow peace of the Dorset countryside.'

This was more than just a fleeting sensation, no mere passing gush of sentiment. He and his mother spent three days with Monica, exploring the attractions of the area, and something about those days away from Cornwall, out of the steely grip of the clayworks, mixing with people, breathing in new air, changed Jack Clemo for ever. His moods would still be bleak, his frustrations rampant, the old landscape soon dominant again. But he had now glimpsed beyond his thraldom and would never forget what he had seen on the other side. In his own words: 'I had received a new, almost a psychic assurance that my frustration and loneliness, the whole process of being refined through suffering, were temporary and superficial, that pain was not the true keynote of my life or work. It was as if I knew that when I next entered Dorset my wife would be with me.'

In the immediate glow of that assurance he wrote the poem

that chronicles the beginning of the shift of perception, 'Daybreak in Dorset':

> Fate-ridden land, in Hardy's view,
> Yet every mood I have seen today
> On Dorset's face, each passionate hue,
> Puts my bleak fate away.
> I am purged now
> Even of my purgation: the furnace fires
> Are hot in Cornwall, and cold is the sand,
> But I take the gentler vow
> To sun that ripens when the fierce flame tires.

It is ironic that the first collection of his verse to appear in print after the Dorset experience was devoted almost exclusively to that 'fierce flame' which he now reckoned was beginning to tire. *The Clay Verge* included seventeen of the poems he had written since the first burst of poetic energy in 1945, but by the time it was published in 1951 Jack regretted the unremittingly grey tone of the volume. The last poem in the collection, 'Sufficiency', poses a series of questions to which he had already found the hint of an answer. Where, he asks,

> Should I find my personal pulse of prayer
> If I turned from the broken, scarred
> And unkempt land, the hard
> Contours of dogma, colourless hills?
> Is there a flower that thrills
> Like frayed rope? Is there grass
> That cools like gravel, and are there streams
> Which murmur as clay-silt does that Christ redeems?

Out of the unresolved question he had made fine poetry. Now that Dorset had pointed him towards an answer, Jack worried that this sort of poem gave a less than true picture of his new

outlook. However he was happier with a second collection which appeared later in 1951 called *The Wintry Priesthood*. Here the claylands imagery is pressed into the service of more cool, analytical verses about some of his literary and theological mentors, including Karl Barth, Søren Kierkegaard and D. H. Lawrence.

Jack had long felt a certain kinship with Lawrence's working-class origins and his passionate exaltation of the mystical role of the senses. But he believed that Lawrence had only seen half the picture, and in his poem 'The Two Beds' he takes him on. In poetry of impressive self-assurance, he employs the clay-working process above ground as an image of the heavenly vision that Lawrence, the coal-miner's son 'groping' below in the darkness, had missed:

> . . . You never saw
> The clay as I have seen it, high
> On the bare hills, the little breasts
> So white in the sun, all the veins running white
> Down to the broad womb with its scars.
> And the scars meant, beyond fertility,
> Purgation—symbol of the stained rock,
> And the live water searching, cooling
> Along the bare sinew; and then the heat,
> The brief heat beyond the body; and at last
> The cup for the new wine. (But that is yonder
> And this is faith.) So I had the open view,
> While you groped in cramped seams, found no heavenly clue.

The Wintry Priesthood won Jack an award of £100 in a Festival of Britain poetry contest organized by the Arts Council, and although the raw energy that characterized *The Clay Verge* was largely missing, Jack felt that in this collection he was beginning to explore in a mature way the issue that had preoccupied him since his teens: the idea that sex, as he puts it, was 'a mystical force with a strong anti-Christian bias, . . . yet potentially the point where human love fused most perfectly with the love of God.'

In practice, of course, Jack was still waiting—ever more anxiously—to prove the point personally. His hopes rose for a second time in June 1951 when a letter arrived from a girl he now refers to simply as T. She was a local girl, eighteen years old, who wrote to congratulate him on his Arts Council prize. They had met casually some months previously and Jack had been impressed then by the quiet diffidence of her manner. When she mentioned in her letter that she wrote poetry herself, Jack's imagination roared into overdrive. He wrote back enthusiastically, stressing among other matters of moment that the newspapers had got his age wrong: he was only thirty-five.

While he was waiting to hear from her again, Jack had another attack of eye-trouble. Swirling red spots kept clouding his sight. The specialist at Truro had grave news for him this time, warning him that there was now a serious danger of permanent blindness. It might take five years to develop . . . it might happen sooner.

T. visited him at Goonamarris to express her sorrow at the news and ask how she might help, but they found communication with scraps of paper immensely difficult. When she returned a few days later, they tried again to recapture the affinity they had sensed in each other's letters, but again conversation broke down under the constraints of Jack's deafness. After she left, Jack tried to keep in touch by letter but this time there was no reply. He was on tenterhooks for months, waiting, hoping. But T. remained silent. Jack was left with the dull conviction that his handicaps had cost him romance again.

Perhaps it was going to take the kind of miracle cure that Eileen had earlier demanded to make him acceptable to someone as a potential husband. With mounting despair, Jack took up the suggestion of an Anglo-Catholic friend that he submit himself to the ministrations of a London faith-healer who had been commissioned by the Archbishop of Canterbury.

It was a long and tiring journey to undertake, the furthest Jack had ever travelled from home, and he was full of apprehensions about the step he was taking. But he did it as a gesture of faith and humility. At Paddington Station he and Mrs Clemo took a taxi to a house in Soho where the spiritual healer was waiting for them. His name was Godfrey Mowatt, and Jack was interested to discover that he was himself handicapped—blind from a childhood accident. He put his hands on Jack's head and prayed.

But Jack's spiritual awareness had deserted him for once and, to his great disappointment, he felt heavy and unreceptive. He did draw comfort of a different kind from Mr Mowatt, however, who reminded him that God could heal in other ways. Blind though he was, Godfrey Mowatt had made a successful marriage.

In the course of the next year or two, Jack participated in a number of faith-healing rituals, culminating in a course of 'priestly intercession' from an Anglo-Catholic vicar in Redruth. But even after taking part, with some qualms, in the rite of confession and absolution, and receiving the holy oil on his forehead, there was no improvement to either his hearing or his rapidly deteriorating sight.

Perhaps the worst of it was having to put up with the well-meaning pity of friends who watched his hopes of healing fade and who knew that the disappointments in his personal life were equally acute. The girl T. had never been in touch again and his dreams there were now quite extinguished. As his foster-sister Frances remarked one day to his mother, ' 'Tis a pity the maids let him down.'

Far from lessening, his infirmities were becoming more severe. In the autumn of 1953 he suffered attacks of cerebral paralysis and heart palpitation brought on, said the doctors, by the long courses of injections he had received for his eyes. For some weeks his life itself was in danger.

One friend suggested in a letter that all his troubles—the handicaps, the romantic disasters, the frustrations of unpublished work—might be a sign that his vocation in life was to be a sufferer, 'a man sustained by grace alone, with all natural pleasures mortified'. But Jack replied with a stubborn denial that his destiny was to suffer. 'I do not at all share your emphasis on suffering,' he wrote. 'There is a truer revelation of God in the least happiness than in years of misery.'

That conviction was about to be put to its most severe test yet.

9

The White Fog

Jack was going blind. After suffering intermittent attacks of pain and inflammation since the age of five, he was now beginning to lose his sight permanently. By 1954 human forms were blurring and both reading and writing were becoming extremely difficult. Nevertheless it was precisely at this time that he started to write a book that turned out to be the most exuberant, even joyful, piece of work he had yet produced—*The Invading Gospel*.

It was initially fired by the 1954 Billy Graham crusade which reached the hearts and souls of so many people up and down the country that year. One of them was Ruth Peaty, who travelled up to London from Weymouth in March with a crowd of friends to listen to the American evangelist at Harringay. Jack was too unwell to travel, but he could still just manage to read the vivid reports of huge and lively crusade meetings, and they excited him. An evangelist himself at heart, he had always thrilled to the gusto and the passion of revivalism.

Now, as he lounged on the settee in the parlour with the crusade song-book in his hands, his heart still weak from his collapse, his sight failing, he seemed to hear again the rhythms of the old Sankey hymns he had loved to listen to in childhood. And somehow, as he recorded later, the music in his mind's ear 'sharpened into an urge to set down a statement of the faith that was keeping me optimistic in circumstances which would have made many people commit suicide.'

That was the idea, but the optimism was hard to sustain in practice. For a start, the sheer physical difficulties of putting words down on paper nearly defeated him at the outset. His sight was now so poor that he could not join up the letters of his handwriting; each one had to be printed separately. The typewriter keys were too indistinct for him to type by sight with his usual two fingers, and he had never learned to touch-type. Mrs Clemo was managing to type his correspondence for him these days, but she was slow and inaccurate. Her own sight was failing as she grew older, and they both recognized that she could not possibly type so much as a chapter for him, let alone a whole book.

So for the time being Jack set aside the composition of the book and concentrated instead on pinning down in note-form the jumble of thoughts that were tumbling through his head, etching them slowly into exercise books in his own hand while a modicum of sight remained.

As his sight deteriorated further, it became increasingly difficult for him to will his spirits into the cheerfulness he demanded. He was determined to write a *credo* based on the insights of joy, not of pain, but these were elusive in the dark hours of 1955 when blindness was pursuing him fast. In an effort to preserve what he called 'a climate of positive faith', he used the last vestiges of sight to immerse himself in the Bible and the Anglican Prayer Book and continued to jot down fragments of *The Invading Gospel* in his exercise books. He made no attempt to write any poetry, taking comfort from the example of the seventeenth-century poet John Milton who had also turned for a time from poetry to pamphleteering. Milton, too, had been struck by blindness, and Jack drew further hope from knowing that he had then gone on to find a wife.

But he was painfully aware that his deafness alone had already cost him dear. What were the chances of fulfilling his romantic destiny when he was totally blind as well? Glib optimism was out of the question. As Jack says: 'My failure to win either Eileen or T. had rid me of all cocksureness about God's will being the established fact at every stage of one's life.' The most that he could attest at this stage was that, through everything, he had seen God's smile. 'Despite the baffling enigmas, the vast stretches of ignorance, the swift and stunning ironies which can follow an apparent miracle, I could only accept the fact that I was still undefeated, that at some point in the testing I had seen in the eyes of God not a tear but a twinkle.'

To be able to accept that at the end of 1955 was a great step forward. By Christmas that year what he describes as 'a white phosphorescent fog' had so clouded his eyesight that he could see nothing through it. For another two years he would still be able to distinguish objects dimly out of the corner of his left eye, but that apart, he was now completely and permanently blind.

The one mercy, for which he would always be grateful, was that his blindness from the outset was white. As a boy, trapped behind his bandages, Jack had known a deep and abiding terror of the darkness. Now, as full blindness overtook him at the age of thirty-nine, he was spared the ultimate horror. His blindness was the colour of the clay-tips. It felt as if he were looking at a giant snowball, bright and light, that had rolled across his field of vision. It is still there today.

Jack's thoughts, though, were black. He sat at his desk for hours, quite still, wrestling with the implications of what had happened to him. Time and again his reflections turned to his dark Clemo ancestry. 'My handicaps belonged to the world of my pagan forebears,' he writes. 'I was not sealed off for a life of quiet meditation, but more roughly reminded of the storm of human delinquency—the gutter and the guttering candle, the curses and sniggers on the stairs.'

It was many months before Jack had worked those thoughts through to an extent that enabled him to lift his pen again in positive mood and proclaim his conviction, in heart as well as head, that Christ had cancelled out his fate, rubbed away 'the dark stain of heredity'. His despair was banished in the end not by force of reason or will-power but, as you might expect with Jack, by the stimulation of his emotions.

News had reached Goonamarris of another evangelistic campaign in Britain, this time by an American teenager called Renée Martz. Mrs Clemo passed the reports on to Jack in the only way she could now talk to him—by tracing each letter of every word she wanted to say on to the outstretched palm of his hand. If the letters were impressed firmly and unhurriedly enough on his skin, he could string them together in his head and make sense of what was being communicated. It was a slow, laborious process, but it was Jack's only lifeline to the reality outside his 'silent white world', as he called it, and it enabled him to feel he was keeping in touch.

What his mother told him of the youthful exuberance of the Renée Martz campaign gave Jack's spirits the same kind of lift that he had received from the Billy Graham crusade. He felt himself being drawn back, out of the nightmare, to the blithe, optimistic world he associated with Browning's poetry. The young evangelist reminded him of Browning's character Pippa. Immediately he wanted to write again. He took out the exercise books that had lain untouched for over a year and began slowly tracing words on the paper, forming each letter from memory, using a strip of cardboard to keep the lines straight. Happiness had driven him back to *The Invading Gospel*.

'Here,' he records, 'was further proof that although I might be inspired by "flashes struck from midnights" I could not be inspired by midnights.'

Some weeks later Jack Clemo did an extraordinary thing. He bought a record-player. It was second-hand and it cost him £14 and he announced that he was buying it because he wanted to listen to Renée Martz's singing for himself. For a man who had been virtually stone deaf for twenty years, this was a pretty reckless gamble of faith. For two months the record-player sat there in the living-room and every now and again Jack would pad over to it and play his Renée Martz record, hearing nothing.

Then something happened. 'One day in November, when I had a cold,' he writes in *The Marriage of a Rebel*, 'I blew my nose and felt a squelching sensation deep inside my ear—and I heard myself cough. I hurried to fetch Renée Martz's record, and a few minutes later stood spell-bound, listening to her clear strong voice soaring amid a thunder of jazz. I could not catch any words, but the sounds were loud and incredibly moving after the years of silence.'

That blessed capacity to hear the strains of music, far away, when the record-player is turned up to full volume, has remained with Jack more or less consistently ever since, although no recognizable words from the human voice have ever penetrated his deafness. It was the joy of hearing the young jazzy song of the teenage evangelist, singing her heart out on that first record, that gave Jack the heart to complete *The Invading Gospel* in almost merry mood.

When reading that book—so full of buoyant affirmation that the *Daily Telegraph* reviewer declared on reading it: 'Jack Clemo is a happy man'—it is hard to believe the mental torment that was bound up in its composition. Even the sheer act of getting the words down on paper was an astonishing feat of endurance.

To start with, his mother had to copy on to his palm, letter by weary letter, every word of the notes that he had scribbled as his eyesight failed two years before. He would hold out the palm of his hand and she would peer at the pages of his exercise books, trying to decipher what she could of the scrawled fragments of thought. As he felt the words take shape on his hand, he would memorize them. Then he had to dictate these passages back to her in finished form, and she would copy it all out, chapter by chapter, in her own spidery handwriting and gloriously idiosyncratic spelling.

Mrs Clemo was over sixty now and the hardships she had endured for forty years and more had left their mark. She was not a robust woman but she had a strong will, and that indomitable spirit of hers did not desert her now. She supported her son in perhaps the most daunting physical struggle of his life without hesitation or complaint, not only writing for him but spending seemingly endless hours searching through mighty tomes to check the accuracy of Jack's quotations. Browning, Barth, Lawrence—she toiled through every wordy page of them, hunting down stray references, pinning a phrase here, a verse there. The book was finished at last in September 1957 and accepted for publication by Geoffrey Bles.

The Invading Gospel became one of Jack Clemo's most popular books. It is more instantly accessible than some of his writing, cogently argued and at times mischievously provocative. The 1972 Lakeland paperback edition informs readers in the blurb: 'This book was written when the author, threatened with blindness, felt the need to set down the beliefs which gave him hope'; and that is precisely what Jack has done.

The central idea is surrender, not in Jack's view a matter of stoic resignation through clenched teeth, but a light-hearted handing over of the self—something that he had taken a while to learn himself. The answer he had found at last to suffering is, he declares, 'neither resignation nor courage, but faith in all its fulness—the faith that surrenders, covenants, endures the testing and obtains the promise, thus rooting the whole life unshakeably and eternally in the faithfulness of God.'

The Invading Gospel portrays Christianity as 'an invasion from a world of infinite joy'. Gone are the savage images from the clay poem days of the human creature dragged into the Kingdom against his will by an Excavator-God. The triumph of faith over natural fate is still Jack's theme, but his theology makes room now for the freedom of the individual to resist if he wants, and it makes room, too, for the smile of God. Smile? The God of *The Invading Gospel* positively capers. Christianity, says Jack, is not God's lecture; 'it is His Big Show and His biggest joke.' The really revolutionary thing about Christian belief, he goes on in a memorable sentence, is that 'Truth did not for ever stay on the scaffold: Truth came down from the scaffold, walked out of the tomb and ate boiled fish.'

There was much else in the book, from his views on marriage to his opinions on art as a tool of evangelism, for the reviewers to chew over. They received it with a fairly consistent mixture of admiration for its insights and irritation at the author's 'hot-gospelling' impatience with intellectual exploration. As one reviewer wrote: 'To suggest that appeal to "intelligence" is "always irrelevant where eternal verities are concerned" and to state that Paul stressed "the emotional aspect of faith" is to minimize the hard work necessary to give thoughtful answers to man's difficult questions.'

Jack's super-spiritual ideas about Christian marriage, purely a matter of the imagination as far as he was concerned in 1957, also provoked a good deal of scepticism. His contention was that the basis of attraction between a Christian couple is 'the yearning on her face or the passion in her voice' as the woman bears witness to her faith; which in turn fills the man with 'a great longing to fuse himself with the facet of Christ which she reflects'. Ruth Peaty expressed doubts about this chapter when she came to read it.

The Invading Gospel was not just Jack Clemo's spiritual manifesto; it was in a sense his clarion call for a wife. After it was published, Jack waited with mounting impatience for the woman of his dreams to pick up the book somewhere and respond to that call. He was keenly aware that he had laid himself publicly on the line with all that talk in the book about marriage and a covenant with God for a practical fulfilment of his destiny. But he was now forty-four years old and he had been waiting for a quarter of a century. As he put it in *The Marriage of a Rebel*: 'For twenty-five years I had been sustained and vitalized by the belief that God had destined me for marriage, and that for this very reason the devil had tried to make me unmarriageable.'

His mother too, he says, was praying passionately that he would find a wife: 'not because I must "marry or burn", but because I belonged to that rarer class of men who must marry or freeze.' But the years passed, and Jack got colder.

Jack's reputation as a poet continued to grow, however. He had become close friends with his fellow Cornish poet, Charles Causley, who was a generous champion of his work. Owing much to Causley's good offices, Methuen agreed to publish a tri-partite volume of Jack's poetry in 1961, which would include reprints of *The Clay Verge* and *The Wintry Priesthood* and add a new collection, *Frontier Signals*. Causley suggested calling the combined volume *The Map of Clay*, a title taken from his own poem, 'Homage to Jack Clemo':

97

In the deep wood dwells a demon
Taller than any tree—
His prison bars are the sailing stars,
His jailer is the sea.

With a brain and ten fingers
He ties Cornwall to his table—
Imagination, at battle station,
Guards Pegasus in his stable.

He walks the white hills of Egypt
Reading the map of clay—
And through his night there moves the light
Artillery of day.

Turn, Cornwall, turn and tear him!
Stamp him in the sod!
He will not fear your cry so clear—
Only the cry of God.

The Map of Clay reflects Jack's progress over some fifteen years
from the stern isolationism of *The Clay Verge*, through the more
expansive mood of *The Wintry Priesthood* to the sense of arrival
that characterizes *Frontier Signals*. The poems in *Frontier Signals*
begin in the old clay world, but it is a world that has now been
'reclaimed':

My soul once felt the press
Of the iron track of fate,
The rumbling of the refuse-laden hours,
And the pitiless signals violate
My faith as the vomit spilled.
But now the fanged pit cowers;
Baptismal waters flood the bed of clay,
Fate's workings are stilled.

The poems that end the collection trumpet the same revivalist confidence that had inspired *The Invading Gospel*. The up-beat thunder of the jazz he had caught on the Renée Martz record had lent a new note to Clemo's poetry. In 'Beyond Lourdes', for instance, he has some friendly advice for a fellow visionary:

> Bernadette, on your bleak verge
> You could scarcely dream
> How a jazz-throb gives the ultimate purge;
> How the Cross bends closer to the neon-gleam
> Than to the grim grotto; how a soul unscarred
> By mystic snow and border-stream
> May flash the healthier vision, spangled and starred.

The Map of Clay attracted more attention than any of Jack's previous works and he found himself being hailed as a new and important arrival on the scene of English letters. The critic Walter Allen rounded off an admiring review with the declaration: 'At his best—and he is at his best, I think, in his early poems, the poems of *The Clay Verge*—he has rendered an industrial landscape more completely and more successfully than any other English poet except possibly Auden, and rendered it as the compelling image of his own bleak creed.' Allen adds an opinion shared by many reviewers of Jack's later poetry: 'In these early poems, where the quarrel is still with himself, the language is taut, strong and naked. His recent verse, written as it were from settled conviction, is disappointing. The quarrel is now with others and the verse has become rhetoric.'

But Charles Causley, in his introduction to the volume, makes no such distinctions. For him, Jack Clemo was quite simply 'a man whose make-up includes genius'. The novelist Colin MacInnes declared him to be 'perhaps the last of the inspired, self-taught English working-class visionaries'. And Kenneth Allsop commended him to readers of the *Daily Mail* as 'the Bunyan of this century', adding that 'his power and importance cannot be much longer evaded'.

Jack was gratified by the acclaim. This was literary recognition on a scale he had hardly dreamed of in the days when he was collecting rejection slips by the hundred. But he had another dream, too, and he couldn't help worrying that all the publicity he was receiving might jeopardize his fragile romantic hopes. Journalists were now writing articles about him that emphasized all the wrong things: the 'bleak creed' he had now outgrown, the hermit-like existence, the poverty, the handicaps—above all, the handicaps. He was dismayed to read again and again, for instance, that he had been blind since the age of five. It was bad enough to have been blind from the age of thirty-nine.

Jack dreaded the effect that all these humiliating 'colour-pieces' might have on any woman who had been affected by his writing and was perhaps thinking of getting in touch. Wouldn't such a woman be put off by the picture of a blind, deaf, grey-haired, grim, penurious, clay-bound recluse? He was desperately afraid that, whoever she was, she might not contact him after all.

But she did, at last, at long last, in January 1963. Only her name was not Ruth, it was Mary.

In her letter Mary described herself as an art teacher in her early thirties and said she had been deeply stirred by Jack's poems and his autobiography. This was just the scenario he had always envisaged, right down to Mary's urgent request to visit him as soon as possible. Photographs passed between them; Mrs Clemo described Mary's face as healthy-looking and forceful, but with a dreamy expression. She came from the Lake District in the north of England, but now lived in Devonshire.

The day she arrived to visit they hit it off in an instant. Jack and his mother met her at St Austell station and she immediately took his hand and held it, as if she knew instinctively how important touch was to a man who could neither hear nor see her. At the cottage she picked up Mrs Clemo's means of verbal communication and was soon scribbling messages on his palm as if she had been doing it all her life. Jack could scarcely believe how smoothly it was all working out. He hardly experienced more than a passing twinge of anxiety when she started to tell him about all her plans to change him. She would get rid of that religious narrowness of his that was going to choke him as an artist if he weren't careful; she would help liberate his 'true self'. When she left, Mrs Clemo advised Jack to stop now before he was swept off his feet.

But there was no holding Jack back—or Mary, for that matter. One or two letters, another weekend's visit and a few weeks later, they were engaged. Mary came to stay for a fortnight that Easter and Jack enjoyed for the first time the taste of a fully reciprocated romance. Here at last, he believed, was the fulfilment of God's covenant.

Mary persuaded him to amend all sorts of personal habits that his mother had been trying to get him to change for years. At her suggestion he began to clean his teeth daily, take more baths, wear pyjamas instead of a shirt in bed, and most practically of all, to learn Braille and touch-typing. Out of pride, he had steadfastly refused to have anything to do with Braille in the past; now Mary offered to learn it with him. Soon Jack was reading Braille books, which immediately began to expand his mental horizons again, and typing his own letters and poems. He felt alive, excited, cherished, busy. Together they chose twenty of his poems to be included in the prestigious Penguin Modern Poets series.

But there was a thread of unease running underneath it all. Mary loathed the claylands; she longed for the open spaces of the Lake District. And Jack began to sense that the romantic novelty of loving a blind and deaf poet was wearing off. He realized that she was becoming much more realistic about the practical difficulties involved. In August of that same year, she broke off the engagement, saying she knew now that she could never fit into his way of life.

Before many weeks had elapsed, though, the engagement was on again. Jack, unable to accept her word as final, had written again on his 'special date', 12 September, the anniversary of Browning's marriage. Mary replied, they met again, and all the old feelings were back. Their relationship returned to its former footing and soon Jack was sending her new poems of his to criticize, and trying assiduously to cultivate the more modern style she liked by reading Eliot, Rilke, Hopkins and Dylan Thomas in Braille.

The next Easter Mary took Jack and his mother to visit her beloved Lakes, and he basked in the unfamiliar northern-ness of the scenes that she described on his hand. The next year he went back there, visiting Wordsworth's cottage at Grasmere this time, and it made him smile to realize how far he had travelled from the years when Wordsworth's poetry was as much anathema to him as the natural beauty that it extolled.

But as the months passed, the old pressures returned. Mary's visits to Goonamarris reminded her of the restrictions that life with Jack must inevitably impose. The industrial clayscape oppressed her; Mrs Clemo's overt religious piety grated; the philosophical differences in outlook between her and Jack caused mounting friction. In the end Mary decided there was no way forward but to break the relationship off, this time for ever. A few letters continued to arrive up to December 1966, as Mary did her best to soften the blow. But then, says Jack, 'there was silence, and I could only finger a big pile of love letters which I had never read'.

The loss of Mary after nearly four years was desperately hard to bear. Jack's only consolation was to know that he had loved and been loved, for once in his life, and that however lonely he might be now, his emotional capacity had been permanently expanded and matured. Never again, he felt, could he go back to the old hermit state. 'It was the lonely, starved, immature self which had found the gaunt and blasted clayworks its true home,' he says in *The Marriage of a Rebel*, 'and that self could never revive.'

The new Jack was much more confident and outgoing. The Wimpole Street vision had failed him once again, but his head was held a little higher now. And deep inside, something kept him hopeful. The dream was battered, but intact. Somehow, sometime, she would come.

In the meantime he gathered together the poems he had written since 1961, many of them inspired by Mary, into a collection published later in 1967 under the title *Cactus on Carmel*. A new element this time was the exploration of Roman Catholic mysticism running through many of the poems, but the collection was not one of Jack's best received. Reviewers noted a softer, more positive spirit than had been evident in the greater part of *The Map of Clay*, but *The Times Literary Supplement* suggested that 'greater affirmation here seems to mean a consequent loss of tension, and some of the craggy strength seems to have gone'. The *Sunday Telegraph*, on the other hand, waxed lyrical. 'Mr Clemo,' gushed the reviewer, 'really has that which amid all our cleverness is in worst danger of being lost to us now: a love and feeling for all that lives, springs, responds and can be hurt.'

Jack collected the reviews as usual and pasted them into his cuttings book. There was little else to do during the summer of 1967. Knowing how empty he must be feeling, a well-meaning friend arranged for a Quaker lady to write to him, which she did in a polite, diffident sort of way, but Jack found the contrast with Mary's passionate correspondence unbearable. He was confused, strained and unhappy: fifty-one years old, hopelessly handicapped, and clinging pathetically—as he realized it must seem to everyone else—to a romantic dream conceived in early manhood, a dream of which he simply could not, would not, rid himself.

Then it arrived, just like that, out of the blue—a letter dated 12 September, the anniversary of Browning's marriage. 'Dear Jack,' it began chattily, as if they had known each other for years. It was signed 'Ruth (Peaty)'.

10

The Courtship

Ruth was not writing, as Mary had, out of familiarity either with Jack's writing or his marriage dream. She knew next to nothing about Jack Clemo. She simply liked writing letters.

She had always spent a good deal of her spare time scribbling epistles to all and sundry: friends, acquaintances, pen-friends, and now and then complete strangers whom she had heard were 'interesting people'. When her curiosity was tickled, or her mind challenged, Ruth Peaty just reached ingenuously for her pen and started up a correspondence. Writing was an outlet for those aspects of her personality that remained largely untapped in her church circle in Weymouth. Ever since the collapse of her hopes of marriage in 1954, she had been thinking and reading on a level that few of the people she knew could, or cared to, share. She was still cynical about glib assertions about 'God's will'. She and her marine seemed to have got it hopelessly wrong; she scarcely knew what she was supposed to think about spiritual guidance and divine direction any more.

Her pain and confusion were compounded by the anguish of watching the slow decline of her beloved brother, Jack. From a handsome, healthy teenager, clever and artistic and full of promise, he had deteriorated into a mentally-ill adult, plagued by increasing symptoms of schizophrenia. He was in hospital now, and it was a deep and abiding sorrow to see him there, so greatly loved but so distressingly changed.

Although her religious questionings continued, Ruth had begun to feel close to her God again as the emotional wounding gradually healed. She lived quietly, working long hours at the laundry, studying her books, writing letters and spending holidays at the Moorlands Bible College in Devon. All her mental energies were directed towards understanding her faith better, making sense of her experience. She eventually felt confident enough to dedicate herself once more to the God whose ways she still at times found hard to understand. She wrote privately one day that 'the greatest lesson of all' had been borne upon her: 'that it's not a case of striving to live for God, but more a matter of surrender, giving our wills to him, yielding ourselves unreservedly. Then it is that the power of Christ can flow through us as a channel.'

One or two men of her acquaintance pressed their suit from time to time, but Ruth was not interested in romance. The memory of the love she had known as a girl of twenty-three still hurt, even after all these years, and she felt she could never be satisfied with less. It would need to be something very special indeed to tempt Ruth Peaty again towards marriage. In time she began to wonder whether that 'something special' might not be a different sort of love from the heady youthful intensity of her early romance; more of a vocational partnership perhaps. She knew that her mother had married the second time out of a sense of vocation and the idea intrigued her. What if she were being slowly prepared—*very* slowly, she sometimes thought glumly— for a similar destiny? She says she began to pray, quite specifically, 'that God would send me a partner in life with whom I could work to serve Him.'

But there were no such worthy thoughts in her head on 12 September 1967 when she picked up her pen to write to Jack Clemo. Far from it. He was simply a name passed on by one of her many correspondents who knew she was on the look-out for challenging books and interesting people. She was still struggling with questions such as why God allows tragedy, and the friend told her that *The Invading Gospel*, by a blind and deaf poet called Jack Clemo, had a whole chapter on just that problem.

Ruth settled down to write her letter in the chair by the bedroom window at her home in Southlands Road, glancing out as she always did at the lovely big lilac tree in the garden. How could she know that by the time it next blossomed she would be declaring her love to this man? Nor could she have had any idea, as she scribbled 'September 12th 1967' of the electrifying effect that date would have on the recipient.

It never occurred to her to write 'Dear Mr Clemo'. 'Dear Jack' just seemed to come naturally, like the impulse to sign herself 'Ruth', with her surname added as a mere afterthought in brackets. The letter itself was scarcely a momentous piece of writing. She wrote in a direct, naively impulsive style that was very much her own:

> Dear Jack,
>
> A correspondent has given me your address so that I can contact you if I wish to. I think you are an interesting personality and I would like to know more about you and how you came to be like you are etc. What are your thoughts on God and the realities of life? I have not read your book *The Invading Gospel*, but I should like to do so. I hear you write poetry mostly—I should very much like to see some if I may. I suppose all your correspondence has to be read to you by somebody. I should be pleased to hear from you soon.
>
> Yours sincerely in Christ,
> Ruth (Peaty)

The letter exploded into Jack's life a few days later. He had spent the twelfth of September in the way he always did, reading Browning's poetry and love-correspondence, and dreaming of the bride who would rescue him from his own Wimpole Street. The coincidence of this letter, unremarkable in itself, having been written on such a day took his breath away. Besides, he liked the sound of this Ruth. The informality of 'Dear Jack' impressed him. The warmth and eagerness of her style went straight to his heart. He could hardly wait to get lunch over before turning to his typewriter to tap out a reply with the slow one-finger method he had taught himself under Mary's tutelage four years earlier:

Dear Ruth,

It was good to get your warm letter. I would like you to write as fully and freely as possible. You may be sure my mother understands and is very pleased to act as a sort of telephone operator when there is someone speaking my language and will ease the loneliness of my heart and spirit. I should be eager to have your comments on *The Invading Gospel*. I think you will find it speaks for you in most deeper issues of life. You may not agree with all I say! As you read, you will get my reaction to the Bible, to Nature and Art.

Yours in Christ,
Jack

If ever there were an encouraging reply, that was it. Jack's letter was hotly pursued by a copy of *The Invading Gospel*, which Ruth began to devour as soon as she received it. The ideas there excited her, and she felt she had discovered at last that combination of mental stimulation and spiritual intensity that had eluded her for so long. Only one part of the book bothered her: the section on marriage, where she thought he was being just a shade idealistic. She lost no time in telling him as much in her next letter, in which she poured out her reactions as spontaneously and guilelessly as ever:

Dear Jack,

I am so happy to know you obviously understand me, and will at least be my friend now and for ever, I hope. There is something spiritual between us. I believe exactly the same as you about God having a purpose in one's own life. I am still a bit cynical about love and marriage myself, commenting on your chapter on marriage. After my unhappy broken engagement years ago, I would never approach it in the same idealistic way again.

The main tragedy (remarking on your chapter in *The*

107

Invading Gospel, 'The Rout of Tragedy') in our lives has been our brother Jack, who has been in a psychiatric hospital most of his life. He is thirty-eight now at time of writing, being treated for schizophrenia which came on in his late teens. Yet he had such possibilities. I'm sure you will be able to understand this, after all the pressure you have been through.

My father died through the war, a complaint brought on through the shock of seeing death and dying all around him at the Battle of Jutland, so I've been told by my mother. Being like all of us over-sensitive, he could not take it. I was twelve when he died.

I don't know why I'm telling you all this. I did not mean to worry you with my troubles and perplexity. May we both desire Christ above all.

Yours in Him,
Ruth

Jack replied that the more she revealed of her experience, the more it became clear that they had 'everything in common as Christians'. They wrote once a week to start with, but before long Jack was writing two or three times in the week, letters which Ruth would answer with a mammoth edition at the week-end; overtime at the laundry did not leave her much time for letter-writing in the evenings. It could take Mrs Clemo hours to transcribe Ruth's longer letters, sitting in her armchair beside the fire with Jack on a stool beside her, his hand held out for the message. Now and then his mother would get up to attend to cooking the lunch, then it would be back to the letter. While it was still fresh in his mind, Jack would answer it that afternoon.

He told Ruth early on about his 1950 visit to Dorset and how he had begun to feel that he had been confined too exclusively to the grim clay landscapes and needed to learn from the softer, more tender kind of scenery. That, he hinted, 'should bring me very close to you.'

They exchanged photographs. Jack's were not very flattering

and Ruth was a bit taken aback. She asked him to send photographs showing what he had looked like when he was younger, 'to see if I've guessed right'. Jack obliged. Mrs Clemo described Ruth's picture to Jack as accurately as she could. Jack says: 'I pictured a fairly tall, slim, almost girlish figure with short dark hair, sometimes smiling vivaciously, sometimes deeply serious. Her letters were fresh and spontaneous, showing a rare and complex personality, emotionally frustrated as I was, spiritually restless and unsettled about denominational ties. We occasionally disagreed, but I admired her forthright honesty, and we began to work towards a complete unity on essentials. The correspondence became the main object of my thoughts and prayers before the autumn was over.'

By the end of October they were discussing, in a general sort of way, what they thought of marriage. Ruth asked whether Jack thought that going without a partner in this world would mean an eternal loss in the next. Jack answered meaningfully:

> One cannot imagine Paul's heaven being less complete
> than Peter's; the Scripture says we are complete in Him.
> But just the same as people have different talents, one for
> music, another for painting, so some have a calling for
> marriage—a sort of mystical insight into its deeper sig-
> nificance. And if such persons don't find their true
> partners, their gift and witness are stunted.

Ruth was thoroughly enjoying the correspondence. What had started out as a casual inquiry to a stranger was developing with every postman's call into something quite different. She felt she had found—that old cliché—a 'kindred spirit', and in her last October letter she tried to put into words what their six-week-old friendship meant to her:

> I do not lack Christian friends. I can get real, alive fellow-
> ship any time I like to go out and mix with the keen young
> Christians in Weymouth. The part that I felt was lacking

in my life was the artistic element. That's what thrills me about our friendship, what makes it different to me. Art takes many forms, and with you it is poetry, and I thrill to the fact that you are a poet, Jack, and that you write to me. I can never thank you enough for appreciating art and literature with me, and being an evangelical Christian as well.

Ruth admitted to herself that creeping into their letters already was what she calls today 'that peculiar feeling and deep pleasure that comes with a developing friendship between the sexes, a discovery that the solitary soul in us can hardly believe to be true—that another person can feel at the same moment, under the same influences, exactly what we feel.' Nevertheless even she was taken aback by the directness of Jack's next letter, in which the possibility of a permanent attachment was mentioned specifically for the first time. He wrote:

> I am glad I fill the gap you have felt so long, and I always want to act for your happiness, *if* God leads us to a deeper bond.

'Well, that gave me a bit of a shock,' says Ruth. 'I was still a bit cynical about the "God leading to a deeper bond" sort of thing.' Still, it was clear that they were both beginning to wonder whether they might suit each other in a deeper relationship, and Ruth decided the time had come to take stock. There was no doubting how fond she had become of Jack or how much they had in common, but the practical side of her nature began to reassert itself. To Jack's dismay, she wrote in November:

> I don't know whether I ought to let the attachment between us develop any further. Suppose I could not cope with the situation. Even if nothing more developed between us, I should not like to lose what I receive from our friendship already, and I am glad I help to ease the

loneliness of your heart and spirit, as you said at first. If
you were not blind and deaf, I would feel much happier
letting it develop.

That last sentence sent a chill into Jack's soul. He had heard
sentiments like that before, and they had always proved the
prelude to a cooling-off. He wrote back wearily:

> A man gets tired if a woman keeps him on the treadmill of
> friendship too long.

It was Ruth's turn now to feel the chill. What if she lost him
altogether? Soon, she realized, she was going to have to make a
decision.

In the meantime they continued to fill in the picture of their
earlier lives. At his suggestion she read *Wilding Graft* and also
Confession of a Rebel which, he warned her, 'shows me in the
midst of spiritual and emotional confusion'. Ruth told him about
growing up in London and how she had loved to roam through
Epping Forest, climbing trees, collecting blackberries and fishing
for tiddlers in the streams. Jack said he would think of her from
now on as his wood-nymph, his pixie; which pleased her. She had
once been a pixie in the Brownies, she told him.

She also told him that she felt she had somehow missed her
true place in life. She spoke of how strongly conscious she had
been of the need 'to align my sense of identity with love and
service'. On 29 December Jack wrote back, throwing caution to
the winds:

> Don't say you have missed your true place in life.
> Your vocation might be rather in sharing the free,
> unconventional life of a Christian poet and mystic. You
> at least keep my mind from becoming musty, and that
> in itself is a good service even if it is not in itself a
> vocation.

When Ruth received that letter, she was in bed with flu. 'That blessed flu,' Jack calls it now, because the period of enforced inactivity over Christmas and New Year gave Ruth a long time to think things out. Jack's suggestion that her vocation might be to marry a deaf and blind poet made a tremendous impact. She was conscious of sharing with him a sense of unfulfilled longing, and reading his poems, as she did every day, increased the feeling of kinship.

'That Christmas,' she recalls, 'when I was reading his poems, especially "Intimate Landscape", the one where he says "Oh darling, lead me safely through the world", something was suddenly released in me. All the pent-up emotion and frustration and betrayal of years was opened up and I cried as I never cried before.'

Early in January 1968, she told Jack about the experience. Jack, who had always hoped that 'Intimate Landscape' would have this sort of effect on a woman, was delighted. He replied:

> I am so sure that this lifting of the veil was meant to
> be—and a real blessing and pledge.

This was the turning point. Each had now tacitly acknowledged a desire to commit the future to the other, and as letter chased letter with more and more confidences they were soon hinting at the idea of a secret wedding like the Brownings'. But there was one stumbling block—and it was a big one. As Ruth says: 'We had to wait and see how we reacted to each other in the flesh. We knew our minds, hearts and spirits, souls and whatever other dimensions of personality there are. But for marriage that is not enough. The test was to be our meeting in the flesh, face to face, hand in hand.'

But with work at the laundry so heavy these days—a new firm was in the process of taking it over and nobody was allowed time off—it would be summer before Ruth could make the crucial visit. So for the time being they had to rely on more letters. Jack started to send her little rhymes to cheer her up on a Monday

112

when she was regularly smitten with back-to-work blues. One of these fun ditties went like this:

> If only you lived at Plymouth
> Instead of near Portland Bill,
> How the bright weekends
> Would make amends,
> How Mondays would flash and thrill.
>
> We feel we are going steady
> Because of the postman's knock,
> But a Poet Laureate
> Must sit and wait,
> Our laundry lass watch the clock.
>
> Still she can sing while she watches
> And he can rhyme while he waits—
> New worlds have spun
> Since the summer sun
> Mocked at our drooping fates.

Now that a spring sun was smiling on them, the tone of their letters became progressively more intimate. The image of the Epping Forest pixie which had so tickled Jack's imagination became one of his most loving endearments. In one letter he wrote:

> Now, my own sweetest Pixie, let me put a song in your heart for ever and an extra glow of sunshine on your face. I love you wholly for yourself, for the wonderful complex nature that no one else recognizes. You must surely feel the warm glow of spring sunshine stealing up from a little cottage where your darling Jack sits and taps his way to your heart.

And Ruth wrote back with equal fervour:

113

Your personality turned Godwards makes you extremely attractive to me. In fact your personality has so gripped me that I have hardly given a thought to the fact that you are handicapped.

At Goonamarris Mrs Clemo was still transcribing every word of Ruth's letters on to the palm of Jack's hand. As soon as the postman called at the cottage around 10 a.m., Jack would pull up his stool to his mother's armchair to get the latest news, although if Mrs Clemo happened to be doing the washing at the time he had to wait. This would leave him in a frenzy of impatience, sitting there with a lovely fresh letter in his hand, opened, caressed, tested for size, everything except read. He had never noticed before how long it seemed to take to wash the clothes. As their friendship deepened, Ruth scarcely gave a thought to the fact that everything she wrote would be seen by Jack's mother, their 'telephone operator'. She felt instinctively that Mrs Clemo 'understood', and in any case she was heartily glad that someone was checking Jack's letters before they went out. When his mother did not keep a close eye on the envelopes they had been known to turn up at the wrong house in Weymouth. But it was a matter of pride for Jack to add a private message in his own handwriting at the bottom of the letter itself, after his mother had scrutinized it as well as she could for typing errors, and Ruth cherished these often illegible love-notes as much as anything in the letter.

On things of the spirit, Jack and Ruth found themselves remarkably in step. On more material issues, however, the affinity rather broke down. Since Jack thought out most of his letters over lunch, it is perhaps little wonder that his mind began to stray in time to future culinary arrangements. Questions like 'Can you cook?' began to crop up with alarming frequency. Ruth replied to that one with a joke that was really only partly a joke because cooking had never been her forte . . . that she couldn't so much as boil an egg. 'I thought he might as well be warned that I wasn't the domesticated type at all,' she says today. 'Well, Jack got very upset and put out, and the next moment he's writing "The poor poet will get thinner every day with no cooked or proper food!"—which got me very annoyed.'

This was only the first of many a clash on domestic subjects. Jack was as anxious about the continuation of a comfortable household routine as any bachelor in his fifties who has been waited on hand and foot all his life. But Ruth had been a working woman since her teens and Jack's unabashed chauvinism made her blood boil. As she says: 'When I got letters from Jack saying I should be more domesticated, I would get furious and say to my mum, "It's all off. I'm finishing with him. Good job I've found out in time that he wants a domestic home-help, not a wife to inspire him." Of course his next letter, being full of love or saying I had inspired a couple of lines of a new poem poured oil on troubled waters, and I found I still loved him as much as ever and could never give him up, no matter what he said.'

And indeed it is that growing love that really shaped their correspondence as spring became summer and the day of their meeting drew nearer. The letters show both of them constantly looking for ways to express what they both felt to be the satisfying 'wholeness' of their relationship. With a few domestic exceptions, whichever area of the other's life they stepped into, each found understanding and sympathy. They kept experiencing the tingle of excitement that comes with the discovery of yet another instinctive bond. Jack felt that his complexities were at last understood and the dominant interest in his life—the interaction of love and faith (or as he had used to put it, sex and theology)—was shared. He began to feel as if he were coming home. In one letter he wrote simply:

> Your letters make me love you with a completeness I never knew before.

But their love could not be complete until they met. They both knew it and they both knew that on the outcome of that meeting everything would depend. They fixed it for June, when Ruth was at last allowed to book a week's leave from the laundry. Jack sent her a rhyme a few weeks beforehand to commemorate the occasion:

> There was a nice pixie from Epping
> Who saw herself nervously stepping
> To a cottage of clay
> On a warm summer's day
> Where a poet sat needing her pepping.

As the week of the fateful visit approached, though, there was nothing nervous about the tone of their letters. Quite the contrary. They were utterly confident. Jack wrote:

> The thrill of touching will be an eye to me that picks out more than words could tell.

And Ruth wrote, even more blithely:

> Isn't it marvellous, Jack? We both feel the same way about everything. When we leisurely climb up Bloomdale Barrow, I shall feel everything you have ever felt.

Neither of them had any inkling of the nightmare they would have to pass through before they could climb Bloomdale Barrow together.

11

The Meeting

Ruth and Bella, who had taken a week's holiday from the office
to be on hand with moral support, set off for Cornwall in high
spirits and booked into a guest-house at Porthpean, a few miles
outside St Austell. This was an adventure. They were to join Jack
and his mother for tea at Goonamarris on the Sunday afternoon,
and Ruth's breezy confidence held out until about lunchtime that
day, 23 June 1968. Then she began to get scared.

They had lunch at the guest-house and stepped out to look for
the bus to St Austell, two women in their early forties but
looking—as everyone always told them—much younger. Bella
was wearing a flowery frock in pink and blue with a cardigan over
it. Ruth, her hair specially 'done' for the occasion, was in her
primrose-coloured suit, an outfit she especially liked. She was
sorry to have to cover it up with her old brown anorak because it
was cold for late June. But then, she remembered, it was not
likely to make much difference to Jack.

At St Austell they changed on to the green bus that they were
told would take them within a mile's walk of Goonamarris. It
crawled interminably up the hill and out of the town, a grey-
looking place on this sunless day, the houses neat and drab. As
the countryside opened up around them, they passed trees and
farmland, straggly hedgerows, a few cows, a speck or two of
sheep. The fields looked tired and dusty. A train rumbled past in
the distance. Then the bus rounded the corner at Foxhole and
suddenly Ruth saw them. 'Look, Belle,' she all but yelled at her
sister. 'It's his tips.'

Jack had tried to prepare her for this moment. He was terrified
that she would be shocked by her first sight of the claylands and
by the memories it would stir in her of his poetry at its most dark

and sombre. That was not the frame of mind he wanted her to be in when they met. So he had warned her to be ready for them, and to a degree she was. But it did not stop her heart lurching with a mixture of fear and awe the moment she saw it all stretched out there before her, a wilderness of clay pyramids, more strange and unearthly than anything she had ever seen in her life before.

There was no time to drink it all in now, though, because she had just spotted a signpost bearing the name of their destination, Nanpean, much earlier than they had expected. She and Bella clattered off the bus in confusion. It turned out to be a stop too early, and there was nothing to indicate the way to Goonamarris. The first person they asked didn't know where it was; the second said 'Down that way', pointing to a lonely, unprepossessing sort of road opening off on the left. They set off towards it.

This was the road that Jack had once called his 'Via Dolorosa', the route, scarcely more than an overgrown lane, between Goonamarris and Nanpean along which he had so often stumbled in his teens, blinded by tears of ecstasy or despair, in pursuit of young Evelyn. Ruth's mission today, in a sense, was to redeem the Via Dolorosa, although she couldn't help thinking that with every step it felt more as if it were becoming hers. The view depressed her. The thought of what lay ahead frightened her. How *could* she have written so airily just a few weeks ago, 'Your personality has so gripped me that I have hardly given a thought to the fact that you are handicapped'? She thought of it now. What would he look like? How would he sound? What if it were all a mistake?

'Bella, listen. I can't go on,' she said suddenly, gripping her sister's arm. Bella took no notice. ' 'Course you can.' They went on.

Ruth tried to concentrate on the road—a yard full of scraps of excavating machinery on their left, then a sluice with water the colour of milky tea. The hedgerow on either side was ivy-laced and splashed yellow with gorse. There were buttercups in the grass verge. As the road began to incline slightly, she caught a glimpse of long grey buildings and mysterious chimneys, while

118

over there on the right the clay-tip that Jack had written about so often loomed into view. That must be Bloomdale Barrow. The idea of a romantic walk up those furze-splotched slopes was already losing its appeal.

Pull yourself together, Ruth, she kept telling herself; you're nearly there. The road was rising steeply now. Jack's cottage, she knew, was just out of sight beyond the brow. And then she caught sight of the two figures. They had just rounded the corner at the top of the hill and were moving slowly towards the sisters, arm in arm. Bella's first thought was that they looked rather pathetic. Ruth was too busy straining to distinguish Jack's form. As they drew nearer, she could make out his smart Sunday sports jacket and flannels, his neat tie. He was bare-headed, thin grey hair wispy across the crown of his head. He looked smaller and slimmer than she expected, and older perhaps than his fifty-two years. His glasses were very black.

On his arm was a figure she knew must be his mother, stouter than Jack, her clothes dark, everything neat as a pin. Ruth watched the couple stop, only a few feet away, and the old lady bent to trace a message on Jack's hand. He waited. Ruth and Bella reached them and they all shook hands. Jack smiled and whispered a greeting and was silent.

Ruth has never forgotten the awfulness of that moment. She opened her mouth to babble greetings and news, she looked into his face to exchange a first shy lover's smile with the man she had been addressing as 'darling'—and she suddenly realized that she couldn't, that she had no idea, no idea at all, how to begin to communicate with him. It crashed on her: this was what it meant to be both deaf and blind. Awkwardly she took hold of his arm and squeezed his hand—the only thing she could think of to do—and the four of them began to walk slowly up the rest of the hill and round the boomerang bend to the grey, slate-roofed cottage on Goonamarris Slip.

Jack felt as if he were walking in a dream. He had spent the morning in earnest prayer, all too conscious that momentous issues were at stake this day. He only managed to pick at his

119

Sunday dinner and kept touching the hands of his glassless wrist-watch to check how much longer there was to wait. Not long after the dishes had been cleared away, Mrs Clemo began to steer him towards the door and then out and down the hill towards the Nanpean bus-stop.

'We were a bit tense,' he recalls, 'but trusting God with the outcome. When Mother stopped and wrote on my palm "Here they are", I stood and waited, trying to look natural and happy until I felt my hand clasped by Ruth's warm, vivid fingers. They were not trembling, and my confidence deepened. She took my arm and we all walked back to the cottage. At times it all seemed like a dream to me—that this "stranger" holding my arm was the "darling Ruth" to whom I had been writing virtual love letters for several months past. I hardly spoke a word, but I was aware of the grim industrial ugliness around us and longed to assure her personally that I had outgrown it as a symbol of my own emotional state.'

By this time Ruth was paying no attention to the industrial ugliness and she barely took in the wild profusion of yellow lupins at the corner, or the hulk of Bloomdale clay-tip dwarfing the cottage, or the pocket-sized garden where Mrs Clemo's early roses were just beginning to bud. All she could think of was this silent man beside her. His appearance had been a bit of a shock, his voice so strange and husky. Of course she had always known in theory that the reality must be something like this, but his letters had always blown the image of handicap far away. He had sounded so forceful and talkative, bubbling with cheek, poised to whirl her off her feet in a moment. Yet here he was, so slow, so worn-looking, so fragile almost. And so very quiet.

Inside the cottage she tried not to look too curiously at the home where Jack had lived all his life. She knew it had changed over the years. The success of *Wilding Graft* had enabled Jack and his mother to replace the old Polmounter furniture in the living-room. Only his desk remained from earlier years, the desk at which he had written everything from the youthful out-pourings in the *Cornish Guardian* to his recent letters to her.

The walls, which during Jack's childhood had displayed Victorian pictures and pious texts, were now hung with portraits and photographs of Jack and his heroes: Jack as a healthy, bright-eyed four-year-old peering over his mother's shoulder; an adult Jack looking dark and mysterious in an artist's portrait; Robert Browning with a beard nearly down to his waist; Billy Graham showing a lot of teeth. There was a record-player in the corner and a big pile of Braille books on one arm of the two-seater settee under the window. It was a cramped little room, but cosy.

When Mrs Clemo disappeared into the back-kitchen to make tea, Ruth followed to help. Mrs Clemo lost no time in speaking her mind. 'Now Ruth,' she said, and Ruth noticed the strong Cornish accent, 'if you don't want to go through with this, you tell him straight away. I don't know that the pair of you were very wise to go talking so much about love in those letters of yours.'

Ruth took the point. She was beginning to wonder that herself. Mrs Clemo led her back into the parlour and seated her beside a still-silent Jack on the settee. 'Look,' she said, reaching for her son's hand, 'this is how you do it.' She traced a word on his palm with a firm forefinger, one capital letter at a time, with a dot to indicate the end of the word. 'Now you try.' Ruth could never remember afterwards what she tried to write on the palm that Jack offered her. All that she remembered was the blank look on his face as her finger flickered nervously across his hand. He looked straight ahead, and she tried again. Nothing. She felt like crying.

Bella was meanwhile keeping up a valiant conversation with Mrs Clemo, and Ruth eventually abandoned Jack's hand and managed to force down a cup of tea and a cake. Mrs Clemo's announcement that they were all to go to the evening service at Trethosa chapel brought general relief. Jack was still not in the habit of attending much, but he wanted to be there that night with Ruth. She found the service relaxing. Without the pressure to talk, much of the tension of the afternoon drained away and they sat side by side in the chapel pew with their shoulders touching in comfortable intimacy. Back in the cottage she gave him an affectionate kiss while Bella and Mrs Clemo were in the kitchen, and they hugged one another in mute reassurance.

When the visitors had left, Jack's mother hurried over to him and wrote firmly on his hand with the rough finger-tip that was so different from Ruth's light touch: 'I like her! I believe this *is* God's move.' But Ruth herself, walking back along the 'Via Dolorosa' to catch the bus at Nanpean, was full of foreboding. She couldn't help noting that the only word she had communicated successfully on her lover's palm that day had been G-O-O-D-B-Y-E.

The next day was infinitely worse. Ruth returned alone to the cottage, determined to make a go of it this time. She had brought her photograph albums, and she sat down beside Jack with every intention of chatting brightly about her family and their home and Weymouth and the sea and the laundry and all the other topics with which her letters had bubbled. But it was no use. 'You tell him,' she had to say again and again to Mrs Clemo, as her nervous forefinger on Jack's palm evoked no response. Mrs Clemo obliged. 'Nice, nice,' Jack murmured politely. Then he turned to his mother, his voice edged with frustration, and said, 'Now let Ruth try.' Ruth did try, again and again, but the tension made her finger dance and Jack, uncomprehending, sat like a statue.

The afternoon dragged on, the photograph album lay discarded and Ruth's tears were not very far away. Her Cockney garrulity had never been so repressed—and with the one person in the world with whom she most wanted to talk. She sensed that Jack was feeling as helpless as she was, but their little touches of tenderness were strained and slightly embarrassed now. She left the cottage in such a state that she took the wrong road and nearly missed dinner at the Porthpean guest-house.

Ruth spent the evening in a state of deep depression and utter dejection. She felt sick. As she sat in the bedroom reading all Jack's letters over again, she simply could not see a way ahead. She loved him and he loved her, but that was not enough if they

122

could not communicate. They could hardly spend their lives passing notes through his mother.

That night Ruth prayed with baffled desperation for a solution. Jack's great vocation for marriage, where was it now? Their shared conviction, deep, deep down, that God had had a hand in their strange courtship, was it all a horrible mistake? And dear God, Jack had believed in this for thirty years; what would it do to him to be baulked again?

When she eventually climbed into bed, Ruth told Bella that she was sure of one thing: tomorrow would decide everything. If she were still unable to get through to Jack, she would take that as the sign that their marriage was not meant to be. Unless her finger could discover the secret of how to speak to Jack's hand, she would leave for Weymouth and not return.

The next day was Tuesday, and Jack waited in vain for Ruth to arrive at the usual time. He too had had a restless night and he went out for a walk to clear his head, groping his way up the lane and trying to prepare himself for the blow that he felt must now be imminent. He wondered how she would do it. Would it be a brief note saying it had all been a mistake and the relationship must end? He could almost write it for her. He returned to the cottage and sat down, feeling stunned.

It was the draught that alerted him to the opening of the door. Someone had come in. Jack sat stock-still, hardly daring to breathe. Then, in his own words, 'suddenly there was a light tap on my arm, a kiss on my cheek. I sensed a difference: Ruth's tension and embarrassment had gone; she was relaxed, bright and positive. Her finger was steady on my palm as she explained why she was late, and to my joy I found that I could follow what she was writing.'

Ruth can't explain what made the difference. Somehow, she says, despite the dark rings under her eyes and the trauma of the night before, she entered the cottage feeling totally confident. That confidence transmitted itself to Jack's palm—how, she has no idea. All that she knew, all that either of them knew, was that their prayers had been answered and they could talk. Her finger

123

chattered away blithely for the rest of the morning. Even the Cornish pasty that Mrs Clemo presented her with for lunch could not dispel her euphoria, although it did take her aback considerably. It was a monstrous thing, served dry without vegetables in the traditional way, and it took all Ruth's stock of politeness to force it down.

But the pasty was soon forgotten in the pleasure of conversing with Jack afterwards, and it was not long before he sensed that the right moment had come. 'Will you marry me, Ruth?' he asked. Ruth, too, had sensed that the time was near. She recalls: 'Knowing all there was between us, I thought to myself that I couldn't possibly say no.' She took his hand and scrawled Y-E-S in huge emphatic letters. And that was that. They sealed their pledge with a kiss and set the date for the wedding.

Jack gave her money to buy an engagement ring. He was never very keen on other people wearing jewellery because it interfered with the impressions he was able to get through touch. As a matter of fact, he and Ruth had debated the matter with some heat in the course of their correspondence. But he knew how important it was to her to have an engagement ring, especially as she had gone without the last time. So she trooped off happily to St Austell in heavy rain the next day and came back with a ruby (her birthstone) set between two diamonds. She gave Jack the box and he took the ring out and placed it gravely on her finger. In return Ruth presented him with a present of her own—a gold-topped fountain pen.

So Wimpole Street had been breached at last, and Ruth went back to Weymouth at the end of the week nursing not only that sense of awed excitement that comes with realizing that you have just committed the rest of your life to another person, but also the special feeling in her case of having accomplished a mission. She, Ruth Peaty, had fulfilled a large piece of the destiny that Jack Clemo had been longing for, and thinking and praying and writing about for thirty years, since the days when she was still a tomboy teenager in London. That long. She carried home with her none of the breezy illusions with which she had arrived in the clay country. Those she had left behind on the 'Via Dolorosa'. She knew now that marriage to a deaf and blind man was likely to be an exacting business.

Jack himself was only too aware of the sacrifices she would have to make. He could offer her neither a honeymoon nor a home of their own. Ruth reminded him wistfully of how joyfully the Brownings had honeymooned in Paris and Italy, but it was not to be. Their honeymoon and their home would be at Goonamarris with his mother. Jack did at least manage to secure a promise from the landlord, however, to modernize the cottage and install a bathroom and indoor toilet.

The letters they exchanged after Ruth's return to Weymouth to prepare for the wedding in October reveal a mutual confidence in their newly established intimacy, and also perhaps a hint of realism that had not been there before. The first of these letters show that neither had forgotten the nightmare. Jack wrote:

> My darling Ruth,
>
> I wish I could write all this with your lovely gold-covered engagement pen, but I guess that would put us back where we were on Monday, when our valiant efforts to communicate ended in sighs of disappointment. I have got to do everything in letters now, but there is a new thrill for you even in my typing, for the hand that touched the key has come to yours and brought you a tender foretaste of our coming Eden bliss.
>
> . . . There is a glow all over the cottage here now, so truly reflecting Browning's words: 'How soon a smile of God can change the world.'
>
> Don't worry, my darling. Just kiss your ring and know that I am with you every moment and God is keeping us every moment.
>
> > Lots of kisses, and all my love in Christ,
> > Ever your own,
> > Jack

125

Ruth wrote:

> Well, darling, everything went as we hoped, after a rather upsetting beginning. I look at my ring and cannot believe that we are actually engaged at last. Wonderful love when it's so spontaneous and beautiful.
>
> Regarding my actual reactions to your physical appearance, I must admit I was terribly shocked at first and I had not visualized properly how it would be, trying to communicate with a blind and deaf man. Still, it is a challenge to me and I have accepted it in love and faith. People will see that true love will overcome any obstacle. I can never hurt you by forsaking you now, even though humanly speaking I am scared at the step I have taken. But I have put my hand in the hand of God and go forward in faith alone.
>
> > All for now, darling. Tender love in Christ,
> > Ruth

The three months before the wedding were filled with discussions about their future life together and the practical adaptations that would be necessary on both sides. Once again the question of Ruth's grasp of the household arts loomed large. As she reports: 'Our few misunderstandings and growing-together pains were mostly over the issue of a woman's role in the home. He expected his wife to be something like his mother, totally domesticated, and I was certainly not that. But he did also say he liked a woman with spirit, so we compromised on the idea of a partnership.'

Jack was not above sneaking in a 'dig' or two in verse, though. When Ruth told him she would need a spin-drier or else he would have to help her peg out the clothes, he hit back:

> Hanging clothes is a feminine feat
> In sunshine or blizzards or fogs;

> If a husband picks up the sheet
> The marriage will go to the dogs.

Ruth had real fears about how she would communicate with Jack. In private she felt she could just about manage the palmwriting, but she was worried that she would be much too shy to do it in public, with everyone looking at her. Jack tried to reassure her:

> When I heard those inexorable words—'I could never make an exhibition of myself by writing on your hand in public'—I could see dramatic consequences at once: see myself falling headlong down steps or stepping the wrong way to board a boat and having to be rescued from the soaking waves. What it is to have imagination! But I don't really feel that we shall let each other down when it's in our power to give happiness in one way or another.

Just over a month before the wedding, first and second class postage stamps made their appearance in Britain. Jack commemorated the occasion with a lament of which William McGonagall himself would have been proud:

> How cruel the Post Office is
> To clap a new tax upon love.
> A letter's as good as a kiss
> But this is too bad, my dove—
> Making us lick a dear stamp
> Or suffer the pangs of delay,
> Our darlings going mouldy and damp
> While we sigh, 'No letters today!'

But the time for letters was coming to an end in any case. Ruth had given her notice at the laundry and came away with presents of a chromium teapot, jug, sugar basin, and some fruit spoons. She was sad to leave after twenty-eight years; the laundry had been her working home since she was a girl of seventeen, newly arrived in the town, and she had made some good friends there. Weymouth, too, was a difficult place to say goodbye to. It was a wrench to abandon its gardens and its beaches and its balmy climate for grey waste-tips, dry pasties and a house on a ridge so bitterly cold that they called it Vinegar Point.

But she left for Goonamarris in October with one thing unalterably straight in her mind; she was going there to marry not a landscape but a man, a man who loved her and needed her and who had fastened his every hope of happiness upon her. Ruth's feelings as she left Weymouth were bitter-sweet, but when she arrived as a bride at Goonamarris they were predominantly sweet.

On the evening before they were married, Jack presented her with a poem. He may have written better in his time, but never with more feeling, never so personally. 'Wedding Eve' is Jack Clemo's grateful, triumphant love-song to the woman who was about to fulfil his destiny:

> Chrysanthemums scent the empty chapel
> On this last night of my unpartnered bed:
> There, foam-like under the dark cliff
> Of the pulpit, they blend their stiff
> Thick tufts with an unseen swell,
> A tide absent when most men wed.
>
> October hush enfolds
> The fruits of a creed's battle, of a bond
> More real to me than time.
> Pews rest in starlight and the hills climb,
> Dune-muffled, to this house which holds
> The crisp ring and the key beyond.
>
> Elect for marriage—I sang
> That stubborn theme through three decades
> Of hunger, mirage, avalanche:

128

When nature made hopes blanch,
A text like a clay-bed tang,
Like the bride's own breath, stirred in the shades.

Forest shade woke you—green boughs,
Fanned sky; then bombers, London's clash,
Splintered your vigil and you fled west,
Prayed under palms and pressed
The white chalk cliffs that spurned the vows
Of your nymph-ardour and dogma-flash.

That Epping trail had to wind
Slowly to my Bethel blooms—no mask
Of dead dreams: tomorrow the grey
Organ-mirror reflects the crowning spray.
Some brides have been tricked, made blind
As they basked, but not where *you* bask.

You chose pure heavenly grace
To mirror the image of your man:
No veiled carnality could pass
The test of that altar-glass;
But it showed you a face, my face,
Scarred, yet singing against earth's ban.

To plant the Cross in the nerves
Intensifies the wedlock sun;
Faith's ravaged fibre now revives
Where the blood thrives,
And I feel in your flushed curves,
In your kiss, the world-renouncing nun.

So two more loves are freed,
Outside an age adrift and dark:
Vigils of dune and forest
Set us on the anchoring quest,

And we find how disenchanted seed
Is changed to spirit's Cana-spark.

Ruth cried when she read it.

Saturday 26 October was one of those days that can't make up its mind whether to rain or not. In the end it drizzled in a half-hearted sort of way, but Ruth was so busy rushing through her ablutions at the kitchen sink before the guests arrived that she hardly had time to notice. (The builders had not yet been in to install the bathroom.) She dressed upstairs in one of the little bedrooms, where she pinned cream roses on to her peach-coloured crimplene dress and fastened another single rose in her hair. She smiled to herself as she remembered the trouble it had cost her to get Jack to wear a suit today. After much persuasion he had consented to be taken into town to buy a new one and she thought he looked extremely distinguished in it. It was brown with thin stripes.

The guests who began squeezing into the living-room after lunch were all family or very close friends. Bella and Mrs Peaty were there, of course, and Jack's two foster-sisters, Violet and Frances, with their husbands. An old friend of Ruth's called Albert White had come to give her away and Jack's best man was Charles Causley, fellow poet and staunch ally. Just before 2 p.m. they all piled into assorted cars and drove a mile down the road to Trethosa chapel.

The little chapel was full of chrysanthemums, just as Jack's poem had said. Big yellow balls of autumn sunshine they were, a fitting symbol for Jack Clemo's wedding. Lightly guided on Causley's arm, Jack walked in proudly, his back erect, the hint of a smile playing at the corners of his mouth. He was completely calm throughout this enactment of his life's dream.

It was a simple service. Jack had memorized the marriage vows, and his mother stood behind him tapping his shoulder at appropriate moments to remind him where to speak. 'He spoke the vows,' Charles Causley has said, 'with all the poetry they contain.' Mrs Clemo left no one in any doubts about her feelings

130

as Causley passed her son the wedding ring to place on the finger of his bride. As Jack wrote later: 'This was a great day for her, vindicating the faith she had held tenaciously for thirty years in defiance of the fate that made me unmarriageable.'

They sang 'O God of love, to thee we bow' and 'O Father all-creating', and Mr and Mrs Clemo walked down the aisle and out of the grey chapel on the hill to the strains of 'Jesu, joy of man's desiring'. Jack could not hear the music, he only caught faint vibrations of the organ through the floor. Nor could he see his bride's face, and the glow on her cheeks as she grinned at him proudly in his slender brown suit. But he caught the atmosphere of joy in that place and it oozed into the core of his being.

In his own private account of the ceremony, he says he felt calm and unruffled throughout: 'I felt a deep thankfulness that God had brought me to the goal I had known to be His will for me, and I also recognized my new responsibility to Ruth, who had put her future life and happiness into my hands. I realized my inadequacy compared with a normal husband, but I believed that God had brought us together and that our marriage was in His hand and could *never* break down. As we left the chapel, I thought vaguely of my past associations there—my childhood, sitting with mother at revivalist meetings. Now she was beaming as she watched me walk down the aisle with a Weymouth bride. It seemed miraculous.'

The guests departed, hugging to themselves the memory of a very special wedding. Charles Causley probably spoke for them all in a radio broadcast some years later when he enthused: 'Wonderful experience. One of the best days of my life—Clemo's wedding day.'

Meanwhile the new Mrs Clemo was being led back to the home her husband called in a poem 'the humblest granite cottage in England' to learn how to be the wife of a deaf and blind poet in her mother-in-law's house.

12

After the Wedding

Mrs Clemo was a sweet old lady. She rejoiced in her son's marriage and she was genuinely fond of Ruth. But she had looked after Jack on her own for fifty-two years, serving his lunch promptly at noon, making sure he always had home-baked cakes with his afternoon tea, anticipating within the bounds of their small budget his every need—in short, spoiling him—and it was hard for her to relinquish the role of running his life to a younger woman. For all her gentle ways, Mrs Clemo had an inexorably firm idea of how she liked things done and regarded most of the conveniences of the modern life-style with dark suspicion. Ruth was introduced to an established household routine which included rising early, scrubbing the carpetless floors on hands and knees and producing a delicately moulded pasty at the drop of a rolling pin.

All of which struck horror into the heart of Ruth, whose own mother had done most of the housework in Weymouth with the help of avant-garde aids like carpet-sweeper and corner-shop bakery; heavy washing had gone to the laundry. Ruth had no idea how to wash a sheet, she had never so much as handled a scrubbing brush, and her hostility to the Cornish pasty knew no bounds. Mrs Clemo did her best to initiate her into the art of making one, but try as she might, Ruth could not get the hang of it. Her pasties simply would not close; the vegetables inside were all over the place. When the aunts and cousins came to visit, Mrs Clemo would inform them in a pitying aside: 'She makes them standing up, you know'—as if that explained everything.

What Ruth describes as her first real victory was winning her mother-in-law's approval for a carpet, instead of rugs, in the living-room. Her next aim was to get it hoovered, a campaign

132

which drew on all her resources of persuasion and negotiation because vacuum cleaners belonged to that considerable range of mod cons which Mrs Clemo designated as 'worldly'. But Ruth won the point in the end. She got her vacuum cleaner, and by the time she had achieved her next goal—a spin-drier—she felt well and truly decadent.

It was for the most part a gracious battle of wills, with both women doing their best to adapt lovingly to new ways. In some respects it was probably more difficult for the old lady, who had found herself suddenly redundant from her life's work. But for Ruth, fitting in with Mrs Clemo was an additional strain at a time when she was having to put in a great deal of effort to the practical business of learning to be a wife to Jack.

The reality of living with a blind and deaf man hit her in little ways. To start with, it depressed her to have no one to dress up for; Jack could not know whether she looked smart or dowdy and she had to fight the temptation not to bother. Eventually they overcame that problem by making a fun ritual out of her descriptions of what she was wearing each day, a game that extended to night-time. She would give Jack a tuck-by-frill account of the nightdress she had on that night, and then describe his own pyjamas to him. 'The striped ones tonight, Jack.' Jack would imagine it gravely.

Jack appreciated that it was in some ways more difficult for Ruth to come to terms with his handicaps than it was for him. His own way of coping was to think of them as something external to his real life, like spots of dirt that had got on his clothes while he was walking home, as he once put it. 'The spiritual world was the reality,' he says, 'and my awareness of it was stimulated by every normal physical pleasure. Ruth was more conscious of what I was missing than I was. "If only he could see my face and the light in my eyes! If only he could see the lovely colour scheme I've arranged in the bedroom! If only he could hear me speak or whisper to him!"

'I did indeed wish I could see and hear Ruth and be a completely normal husband to her. We could have had many more

133

thrills of "sharing", especially in her beloved Dorset, and I could have relieved the burden of housework at home,' (Ruth grinned sceptically when she saw him type that bit) 'brought her breakfast in bed and so on. As it was, I could do little more than wipe the dishes, attend to the dustbin, weed the path and clip the grass in our tiny garden plot.

'But I had trained myself in positive thinking and considered myself a very fortunate man. I was always thankful that my blindness was a white phosphorescence, not a horror of darkness. My hearing had always recovered in various degrees from attacks of stone-deafness. Tokens of mercy.'

Jack understood only too well what a strain it was for Ruth to be with him day after day, unable to converse. He was remarkably sensitive to her moods and emotions from the first. He could always feel resistance or annoyance or excitement in her finger when she spoke to him, trace sadness in the lines of her eyes, or enjoy a silent joke with her when visitors called and he could feel her back and shoulders heaving with laughter as she sat on the stool against his knees. He loved her all the more for her resilient cheerfulness when he knew how low her spirits often were in the early days. And she loved him the more for understanding.

Ruth quickly discovered what Jack had known for years—that palm-writing is an intensely frustrating mode of communication. It makes conversation slow and fragmentary. Ruth would be bursting to tell Jack something, her finger would move too fast and he would sit there looking blank and unimpressed; that could drive her wild. Sometimes she nearly exploded with the frustration of not being able to get a good retort out when she felt like it. A nicely calculated wifely put-down loses something when it has to be repeated up to three times, letter by letter.

Equally, Jack found it hard when Ruth, in the middle of explaining something or dictating a sentence for him to type, would suddenly dart off to attend to the stove in the kitchen, leaving him trying to work out what she was saying. She did not always remember how maddening it is to be cut off mid-thought or mid-sentence, left in limbo for half an hour or more. But they never forgot how to laugh, and right from the beginning they did a lot of that together, teasing and giggling, deflecting an irritation with a joke or just revelling in the fun of being with one another. As Jack says: 'We often frolicked like children when some happy turn had eased the monotonous routine. We took the moods as they came, and there was the constant comfort of being together amid the ebb and flow of romantic feeling.'

Ruth admits that she did become very depressed at times in the first years. The Goonamarris landscape began to oppress her spirits more and more. At first there was a certain fascination in the novelty of her new surroundings and she even enjoyed the challenge of searching out unspoiled walks on which she could watch for the wild violets peeping out in season, and the foxgloves and the lupins and the vivid yellow gorse along the roadside. But gradually the monotony of the clayscape began to haunt her and she found herself missing the variety of the Dorset colours, the sea, the open spaces. She ached for Weymouth. She used to return from her afternoon walks more depressed than when she set out, and the routine of life in the confined space of the little cottage did little to relieve her spirits.

Two years into their marriage this feeling of claustrophobia reached its peak and Ruth felt she was at her wit's end. She started to pray for a friend, for an outside interest that would complement and feed back into her marriage. It was then that she met a lady from Newquay called Gwen, who had a car. Gwen began taking her out on trips around Cornwall, the pretty, romantic, sea-girt Cornwall that she had barely glimpsed before. The companionship and the fresh air and the regular changes of scenery were like a lifeline to Ruth at that time. 'Gwen was the answer to our prayer,' she says.

Her prayer had been Jack's also, because praying together was grafted into their marriage from the first. They knelt side by side in their bedroom every morning and evening, Jack speaking their devotions, Ruth touching his head with her hand. In that quiet place they brought the tensions and worries of the day to the surface and let them go. Together they would come before the

God they believed had ordained their marriage and felt themselves sustained and guided by the power they tapped there.

Both Jack and Ruth emerged from the frustrations of those early years of marriage with a deeper love and a stronger sense of security than they had ever known. The commitment was absolute, whatever the strains, and the love flowed from that. Ruth found there was a sweet balance in what Jack offered her as a husband. Perhaps he could not converse easily, or compliment her on a new dress, or share experiences in the way she might have liked. But he knew how to make her heart glow, how to reassure her when she felt lost, how to make her feel the most beautiful, wanted woman in the world. And when sorrow came, he knew how to console.

As always, it is in their letters, where no handicap could impede the heart's message, that you find the most moving expressions of their married love. They wrote twice a year, to start with, when Ruth went on holiday to Weymouth to visit her mother and sister. Jack had to stay at home with his own mother, who was now too frail to be left alone or to make the trip with them. During their first separation, six months after the wedding, Jack was writing:

> This morning I simply wanted to go to sleep for eleven days and wake up to find my dear pixie still with me. But we will keep close in thought, darling, remembering the loveliest moments and looking forward to the spring and more honeymoons. Since this time last year how much a pixie has transformed all the heart and outlook of the old clay poet.

By September 1971 ('the sixth time you've done this disappearing trick'), Jack was bemoaning 'the lack of anything to plant kisses on except paper'; his thoughts flitted constantly, he said, to 'pixie in the bus, pixie glimpsing the Weymouth sea, the lilac tree in the garden'. In another letter he said he missed her everywhere. 'Half of me seems to be missing, evaporated or spirited away . . .

136

Now I've lived a whole week without the touch of a vanished hand, but our love and faith have kept warm.'

Ruth's return to Goonamarris each time from these short breaks away would indeed stimulate a honeymoon feeling in the cottage, and Jack often found that the poetry would gush from him more fast and fluent than ever at these times. The happiness that marriage brought him was proving as creative as he had always predicted it would be. In 1971 he published many of the poems written since his marriage in a collection called *The Echoing Tip*. Several of them are in the form of dramatic monologues about characters whose lives he had been studying in his Braille books—people like Katherine Luther, Emily Brontë and the painter Alfred Wallis. Others are directly inspired by, and in tribute to, his wife. One such is the delicately wrought love-poem, 'In Contrast', in which Jack showed that for a man who had by then seen nothing for some fifteen years, his ability to render a scene in precise and vivid detail remained undiminished:

The feet that now pause with mine
Where a winter wagtail chafes the stringy twigs
Above the white slow clap of a clay-land rill,
Were wont to pause where Hardy paused,
His nerve drained of desire,
Hearing gulls gabble, wind whip Portland Bill,
And the heart's vultures shriek round a Cornish spire.

The hand which at last lays mine
On the scarp's meek morsels of bride-white hawthorn spray,
Ferns, whortleberries, culled from a sand-cone's lap,
Has reached, as Keats' hand once reached
In febrile flight from love's stings,
Where the sweet Teign dissolves in the red mouth, flap
Of an ebbing sail seems frail as his nightingale's wings.

Less successful, in the opinion of some reviewers of *The Echoing Tip*, was Jack's handling of more abstract ideas. *The Times*

137

Literary Supplement castigated him for 'an overcharged, over-heated poetry, a thrashing whirlpool of inflated, quirkily un-predictable metaphors which seem selected by no discernible pattern of imaginative logic'. The *Church Times* found his verse 'still angular and sometimes awkward', but added that as auto-biography his poems were 'among the most impressive of the last decade'. The literary magazine *Outposts* was unstinting in its praise: 'A serious poet, writing in serious times, Clemo sounds a deeper note not often heard these days, when sceptics feel safer in shallow waters.'

Jack believed that as a poet he had at last found his true voice. Released by marriage from doubt and confusion, he wanted his idiom now to be buoyant and life-asserting. To those readers who missed, as one put it, 'the tensions of the Genevan lightning rod in the polluting clay', he gave his answer later in *The Marriage of a Rebel*: 'While a poet is fighting desperately to make his vision work, he will mis-state or overstate his case and present a faith bleared by the smoke of battle. This may give his writings a strange originality, but it makes him less reliable as a guide and teacher. It is only after he has demonstrated that his vision works, when he is living it on the everyday bread-and-butter level, that he can say exactly what he means without a false note or a warped emphasis.'

Jack was certainly a new man. People who remembered the truculent, aggressively reserved young fellow of earlier years with his perversely anti-social behaviour and studied lack of interest in his appearance must have been hard-pushed at times to recognize the assured, smartly dressed man of letters who turned up on the arm of his wife at a variety of social occasions.

For a start he went to church. After an absence from the Sunday pew lasting more than thirty years, Jack had begun to worship regularly at Trethosa chapel again. He could catch the vibrations of the organ music through the floor-boards under his feet, and Ruth sat at his side transcribing the gist of the sermon on to his palm. Jack's thoughts often strayed during the service to the poem he was working on at the time, and he enjoyed the irony of composing lines about Roman Catholic saints in a Wesleyan pew. He remained impatient with tepid Christianity, but his marriage marked the beginning of the rebel's reconciliation with fallible Christian fellowship.

Two years after his marriage, Jack did something he would never have done before it. He accepted a Cornish bardship in honour of his poetic achievements, an offer he had turned down twice before he met Ruth. He had little interest in Cornish nationalism, but he realized that the occasion would give Ruth a much-needed break from the monotonous routine at Goonamarris. That is how Jack Clemo came to be 'crowned' *Prydyth an Pry* (Poet of the Clay) at the Cornish *Gorsedd* festival in September 1970. The Grand Bard granted Ruth the singular honour of slipping the large blue hood on to Jack's head herself, conferring on him the mark of bardship. Mrs Clemo senior looked on proudly from the audience.

Jack also started to accept invitations to poetry readings and arts guilds, where Ruth happily and unselfconsciously scribbled an account of the proceedings on to his hand in front of everyone, despite all her premarital anxieties on that score. Jack found himself enjoying a transformed social life. 'Before I married,' he says, 'I had refused all invitations to appear on public platforms or to accept public honours. Having written so much about marriage, I could not face an audience while still a frustrated bachelor.' Now he faced audiences all over the county with his head held high.

In 1973 the smooth rhythm established in almost five years of married life was disrupted by an ordeal for them both that tested the maturity of their relationship. At the beginning of the year Ruth was called urgently to Weymouth by Bella, who said that their mother was acting strangely. Ruth was extremely close to her mother, who understood the difficulties involved in the vocational sort of marriage that Ruth had chosen and who had given her solid support every step of the way. Mrs Peaty was now suffering from the infirmities of old age and from psychological strain brought on by the continuing heartbreak of her son's mental condition. Ruth arrived in Weymouth to find her ill and confused. Jack's empathy followed her there in a letter:

> It's a winter's shadow in every sense, and I know so well how you must feel as I write this, all cold and threatening around you . . . Our love is more deep and tender at times like this, and it is helpful to know that Mum always believed I would be a kind and good husband to you.

Ruth reported back that Mum, as they both called her, was very disturbed. She was refusing to eat and seemed 'so sad and despairing'. Jack waited at home anxiously for news. He found this separation much heavier to bear than the short holiday breaks, but he tried hard to be positive for her sake:

> My own dear wife,
> You can guess how eagerly and prayerfully I have been awaiting your news, and all my love flowed round you when your letter came and I tried to realize what it must mean for you. I miss you so much, darling, but the sacrifice is repaid by the knowledge that you are helping dear Mum in her dark hour and giving her the comfort of your presence.

Ruth was in an impossible position. Her mother needed her and Bella needed her, but so did Jack. Without her, it was like being in his pre-marriage prison again, with the light out. She knew how the strain would be wearing him down and when in one letter he gently encouraged her please to come home as soon as possible, she realized she had to return. In that letter, Jack added wistfully:

> I pray God we may never have this sort of suspense again, or separation. It may refine our love in the furnace, purging it of selfishness, but I still believe that love must also be refined in sunshine. I know more deeply now than

ever that you are the only woman in the world for me and this must mean that happiness is meant for us—not selfish, but a source of strength for helping others.

Mrs Peaty was taken into hospital and Ruth wrote:

What a worry it all is. Your letters have been my main comfort and support. I hate leaving my Mum like this, but what else can I do? I know you are living for me to return, as you said in one of your letters. I can't write any more now, as I'm too upset. See you soon, darling.

Your own Ruth

Ruth returned to Goonamarris, but their life together scarcely had time to resume its rhythm before she was called back to Weymouth. Her mother had been sent home from hospital and Bella had collapsed under the strain of looking after her. This time the crisis had the effect of provoking in Ruth doubts about her marriage. Had it perhaps been a mistake after all? Had she been wrong to leave her mother to marry someone so dependent on her as Jack?

Jack had to muster all his resources of sympathy and self-confidence to allay her guilt and renew her vision of what their marriage was all about.

My own darling Ruth,

Just a little love-note to link us up and make you feel that special and strong tenderness which only a husband can give. You must have felt my love and understanding flowing in, calming and strengthening you on your last visit home, and now this crisis is surely at its peak and we must meet it on the level of the witness I've given through our marriage.

The point where you are tempted to feel that your launching out to share and inspire my witness may have been a mistake—you must not give in to these feelings.

141

The call was personal between God and our hearts and souls, and it can't be falsified or put in doubt by any other circumstance. A missionary might learn that after she had gone to a foreign land her family had run into dark testing times of sorrow or sickness, but she could not question her call or blame herself for obeying it. All our friends know you did right and so does your own mother.

. . . I know what you are facing, my own darling, and my heart aches with the mystery of it. Yet Christian marriage isn't meant to be just personal enjoyment. The Cross must be planted in the nerves sometimes, drawing us deeper. What a strange birthday I shall have on Sunday, the day of sacrifice, but it will bear fruit, please God. I feel the warm glow of having a dear wife still breathing my air and pulsing on my wave-length. God is watching and over-ruling.

The old lady was taken at last into the geriatric unit at Dorchester Hospital, and Ruth felt it was safe to return to Jack. But she was only home a matter of weeks when her friend Gwen arrived with a phone-message. Mrs Peaty had passed away. Ruth rushed back, in an agony of conscience for not having been there, and Jack seemed to reach a new level of maturity as a husband in the spate of letters he sent after her, flooding her with comfort, support, security and a tender encouragement to start rebuilding. After the funeral he wrote:

I longed to be there with you so that you could be leaning on my arm as well as God's . . . Treasure all the lovely happy memories which bring the assurance that Mum herself wouldn't wish you to stay crushed for too long. I shall reach out to you as we sit in our chapels on Easter Sunday. It must surely mark the beginning of an upward sweep towards life and happiness again, after these four months in the dark valley. I miss you so much, darling.

In another letter he urged her to look forward again:

> The last wrench is over and we are free from that awful
> feeling that Mum is up there suffering alone. You can
> come back not merely brave but thankful that there is a
> new life to build up with me in the broad sunshine, and
> even moments of spring-like gaiety, for you'll always be a
> pixie. Try to relax and get everything in proportion, as
> Mum would wish. Happy days ahead.

It was many months before Ruth regained her spirits, but their
marriage was the stronger for the pain they had passed through
together. Jack's next collection of poetry, *Broad Autumn*, published in 1975, glows with mellow contentment. The magazine
Outposts called it 'beyond question Clemo's best
book to date' and added: 'It is as though his personal pilgrimage,
his Cornish and Methodist heritage, his early struggles and
later blindness, his comparatively recent marriage, his lifelong
wrestlings with "tensions of darkness", have now brought him
"in broad autumn . . . a new peace", and greatly enriched his
verse.'

There was one more sorrow to come. Old Mrs Clemo was
reaching the end of her journey. She was in her eighties now,
desperately frail and almost blinded by cataracts. The years since
Jack's marriage had not been easy for her. The erosion of her
role as his sole support had left her confused and a little lonely,
although she bore it with grace. Towards the end of her life she
spent many hours writing a little autobiographical booklet called
I Proved Thee at the Waters. She wrote it in secret, slowly,
painfully and diffidently, but determined that before she died she
would leave a record of the way her faith in God had been
vindicated in her own life and her son's.

Whatever the strains she had suffered as a result of Jack's
marriage, Eveline Clemo had no doubt that it represented a
triumph of faith. His wedding, she wrote, 'was the climax of the
great promise given to me in my darkest hour, "Great shall be

143

the peace of thy children." . . . God has not forsaken us, He has fulfilled His promise to us to the very letter. To have lived to see the results of a simple, trusting faith in the God of love, forgiveness and wisdom has meant an old age of peaceful joy and loving anticipation.'

It must have given her a deep satisfaction to act as 'telephone operator' between the couple during Ruth's Easter holiday in Weymouth in 1976, in what turned out to be one of their last separations. It can only have pleased Mrs Clemo to see Jack declaring that after eight years of marriage, 'my message is vindicated in spite of all adverse winds and clouds and strains and rains, and I think they come to us less than to most couples'. Perhaps she stifled a wry smile when she read him telling Ruth that 'you are such a superb manager of money, cooking ingredients and loose buttons'. But she must have appreciated the clear-eyed insight of the sentence 'We would be on the rocks by this time if we weren't on THE Rock' from the son whose excesses of romantic idealism had once caused her so much worry.

On the night of 3 June 1977, Mrs Clemo slipped quietly from life with as little fuss as she had lived it. Perhaps in the end she simply let go, secure in the knowledge that her son would be cared for in his grief and for the rest of his days, and that her own life's work was now accomplished. The funeral service was at Trethosa chapel and Jack wore his brown striped wedding suit. Charles Causley was there, and in a tribute in the *Western Morning News* a few days later he described Eveline Clemo as 'one of the most remarkable women Cornwall has ever produced'. Without her, he said, a large part of Jack Clemo's poetry would not have seen the light of day. 'She was the instrument through which Clemo—I think a writer of genius—was in contact with the world.'

Causley's words must have been privately echoed by everyone who had had the privilege of knowing that remarkable woman. Where would Jack Clemo be now, everyone was asking, if it hadn't been for his mother? Jack wondered too.

144

At Goonamarris it was the end of an era. Jack and Ruth were on their own for the first time in their married life, and Jack was free to explore beyond the clay country and share at last something of the Weymouth experience that had shaped Ruth's life. Soon the transformation of the Poet of the Clay would be complete. Within a few years of his mother's death, Jack would be able to visit a claywork museum in Cornwall and write afterwards: 'I was entirely unmoved, almost bored, by everything I touched, as if it belonged to a world that had lost all meaning for me. It was associated with a penniless, lonely, self-tortured village hermit, and I could only ask: "Who's that chap?" Jack Clemo and his wife were stroking the palms in Sandsfoot Gardens a few weeks ago.'

13

'Only Solid Peace'

Their first visit to Weymouth together was in the autumn of 1977, and Ruth was overjoyed to discover that Jack immediately 'fitted in'. He told her he could feel her roots as he stepped into the Peaty living-room in Southlands Road and settled himself and his typewriter at the desk which Ruth had placed for him by the window, as if he had been writing there all his life.

Ruth could hardly wait to show him all her special places, especially Sandsfoot Castle Gardens where she had whiled away so many hours, happy and sad, in the past. They rambled all over the gardens, sitting at one wooden bench after another so that Ruth could describe all the different views of sea and ship and harbour. They wandered among the castle ruins and she warned him to watch his step because the ancient flagstones at the bottom of the path were uneven. She guided his hands along the railings and thrust them among the petals of the late summer roses. He felt the palm trees she had talked so much about, strange and spiky to the touch.

Jack said very little, but Ruth knew the impressions were penetrating deep. Later there was a poem, evoking a subsequent visit in the rain. In that poem, 'Sandsfoot Castle Gardens', Jack would make it clear where his allegiances now lay:

> I have questioned often, questioned the worth
> Of the long pain and mirage, the rotten clay-fields,
> Or the cruel fate distorting clay-fields and me.
> I hardly care where the blame goes:
> Five pattering minutes more
> And we shall caress together

The laughing tongue of the palm tree,
The damp full lip of the rose.

Jack felt from the very beginning as if he belonged in Weymouth. After that first autumn visit in the year of his mother's death, he and Ruth returned every year for visits that grew longer and longer each time. He liked the Rodwell house, roomier than his Goonamarris cottage but not too large for him to get lost in. He enjoyed living in a town—yes, Jack the onetime recluse who used to hate meeting people. Now the social contact stimulated him. He also revelled in the access to the natural beauty that Ruth was teaching him to appreciate. Jack had long ago lost the impulse to denounce automatically all that was soft and fragrant; married happiness had sucked the clayworks of their potency.

As he explained once in a television interview, it was not the fact that he could no longer see the claylands that had loosened their grip on his imagination; it was emotional and spiritual maturity that did it. 'I've never dedicated myself to a landscape,' he said, 'only to a faith and the fulfilment of a romantic dream. The faith is mature now and the dream has come true, so I wouldn't go back to harsh industrial images even if I could see them.'

In any case, Jack was never short of a symbol or two to evoke the Clemo condition, even in Weymouth. The very first poem he wrote at his new desk there was about Chesil Beach, a thin scythe of pebbly sand, more pebble than sand, near Weymouth Bay. Ruth took him there early in the first visit. He felt the stones slipping underfoot—'smooth, rounded like eggs'—and Ruth and Bella spent hours back at home patiently explaining the geography of the beach so that he could get the detail clear in his mind's eye. When Jack eventually sat down at the desk to wait for the lines to compose themselves, he found in 'Chesil Beach' a new image of himself:

I am no foreigner here
If one can judge by an atmosphere.

147

This is my birth-image—freak and chaos,
A stammer of stone where custom called for sand.

On their third three-month summer visit to Weymouth in 1979,
Jack told Ruth what she had hardly dared allow herself to hope:
that the Cornish clay poet would like to live permanently in
Weymouth some day. In fact, the move would take another five
years to come about, but from that moment there was no going
back.

In the meantime, life at Goonamarris proceeded uneventfully,
a good deal too uneventfully for Ruth's liking at times, although
her friend Gwen continued to drive over from Newquay on a
Wednesday and take them both out for trips in her car. Jack was
busy working on the second volume of his autobiography.

His mother's death had opened the floodgates of memory;
reminiscences poured out of him without planning or effort.
Every morning he would scrawl a few hundred words in an
exercise book, holding a sheet of card taut against his pen to help
himself to write in a straight line. He would memorize each
passage as he was writing—years of training had given him
prodigious powers of recall—and in the afternoon he would type
it all out. Sometimes he added or altered a phrase as he typed,
but for the most part *The Marriage of a Rebel* as published is his
original draft. Each day Ruth helped him keep the flow going by
copying on to his hand the last few sentences he had written the
previous day, so that he could be sure that the new paragraphs
would fit in smoothly and keep the narrative coherent.

The Marriage of a Rebel, which Gollancz published in 1980, is
Jack's story of his search for a wife, culminating in a discreet
summary of the first nine or ten years of married life. Reviewers
uniformly hailed it as a fascinating tale, although many were
puzzled by the sub-title 'A Mystical-erotic Quest'. The *Church
Times*, for one, felt obliged to assure its readers that 'there is not
the slightest hint of sexual licence or titillation in these pages'.
Jack himself, who had meant to evoke the rather more sublime
associations of the Greek *eros*, realized he had made a mistake.

148

Not for the first time, he had used a word with connotations in the world beyond his cottage of which he had been unaware. That misunderstanding apart, the book was well received. The *Daily Telegraph* said: 'His amorous odyssey has the candour of Hazlitt's, the intensity of Lawrence . . . He writes so well that most readers will probably be absorbed by his obsessions; some may find them at times claustrophobic.' In the *Scotsman*, Alan Bold called it 'this magnificent book'.

Publication of *The Marriage of a Rebel* enhanced the growing celebrity status of the Clemos. The colour magazines sent writers and photographers to Goonamarris and Jack, although appreciating the attention, winced all over again as his handicaps were paraded in exaggerated detail in front of the nation, despite his lifelong efforts to play them down. Television and radio also took an interest in what *The Times* had called 'one of the strangest love-stories of our time' and Jack found himself in the not entirely unpleasant position of being a local tourist attraction.

In April 1980 the BBC screened a drama-documentary of his early life-story. This had been shot in the claylands the previous year with the actor Robert Duncan in the leading role. He is a Cornishman who had grown up in St Austell and knew of Jack from local reputation and from one particular television sequence in which he emerged as a strange and powerful figure crouched in his wild clay landscape. Robert Duncan still remembers that early impression. 'He was just like an angry old ram,' says the actor, 'battering his head against a wall of clay.' When invited to play Jack Clemo in the BBC's *A Different Drummer*, he leapt at the chance to meet the man at last and study his character and the faith that had motivated him. As a result of their contact, Duncan himself came to re-evaluate his own beliefs and became a Christian not long afterwards.

Jack self-mockingly evokes the image that local children like Robert Duncan once had of him in a lighthearted verse in *The Bouncing Hills*, a collection of fun writings published in 1983. It gathers together some of the slapstick dialect stories he wrote back in the 1930s, as well as a handful of rhymes penned mainly

149

in the 1980s for the children he still loves to be around—the sons and daughters of friends in Cornwall and Dorset, and youngsters who had taken part as extras in the BBC filming. These verses are not serious poetry; they are more like the doggerel with which he used to cheer Ruth up in his letters. But they do show what Jack has been at pains to point out in later years: that decades of disappointment and frustration and grim fulmination had not robbed him of a sense of humour:

> You've heard of the Cornish curmudgeon,
> That surly, cantankerous chap
> Who scowled at the flowers in dudgeon,
> Or growled at a kid on his lap.
>
> "How awful to meet Mr Clemo!
> He can't hear a word that you say:
> His speech is restricted to 'Hem!', 'Oh!'
> And 'Yah!' as he drives you away."
>
> We beg to inform all and sundry
> That this is not true of him now:
> His manner has ceased to be thundery,
> He has learnt to say 'Honey' and 'Wow!'
>
> And even in his fame's epidemic
> You'll find him astonishingly calm
> As you hinder his ode or his epic
> By writing small talk on his palm.
> *Epilogue: Chorus of the Children*

Jack's 'fame's epidemic' had now stretched even as far as the halls of learning he once so heartily despised. In July 1981 he accepted an honorary D.Litt. degree from Exeter University. The man who had left his academic institution at the age of twelve because it could teach him nothing he wanted to learn walked forward in the procession of robed graduands, on the arm

150

of his wife, to receive the university's most coveted honour in the Great Hall at Exeter. Then he was taken to the Library to inspect his early manuscripts which he had allowed to be housed there. The happiness of his day was completed by a conversation with the scholar Dr Donald Davie, who told Jack that he had included four of his poems in the new edition of the *Oxford Book of Christian Verse*.

Now that their lives were public property in a way that Jack could never have imagined in the days when his work was un- recognized and his dreams lay in shreds, nor Ruth for one moment have visualized when she picked up her pen to write to just another 'interesting personality', they received visitors and letters and requests for interviews from far and wide. People who had read Jack's books trekked to the Goonamarris cottage on what sometimes looked like a pilgrimage to the prophet. Ruth would always sit at his side and transcribe the visitor's questions on to Jack's hand: questions about life and faith and love and marriage. If they could not come, they wrote, and Ruth would spend a large part of every morning 'reading' the mail to Jack.

Today the mail and the visitors still arrive, but they come now not to Goonamarris but to the semi-detached house in Weymouth with the lilac tree in the garden and the sea a wave's breath away, where Ruth grew into adulthood. Jack and Ruth joined Bella there permanently in October 1984, after closing up the old cottage for ever. Jack's old desk, his bookcase, his cupboard and the ancient dresser that his parents had lugged from the Goonvean farmhouse seventy years before all went to the home of a friend. The rest of the furniture was packed into a van and sent to Weymouth.

On 19 October, mid-afternoon, Jack locked for the last time the door of the slate-roofed cottage where he had lived for almost seventy years himself. He did so without a single pang of sadness, without so much as a last mental look at the house which had been both his Wimpole Street and his Eden, or at the lowering clay-tips which had made him a poet. No, Jack walked stolidly up the garden path, climbed into the van and looked ahead; truly, as

151

he once described himself, 'a poet without nostalgia'.

It was Ruth who looked back as the van drove off, Ruth who realized at the last moment that she would miss the unearthly wildness of the Goonamarris landscape, for all the heartache its bleakness had caused her over the years. She was happy to be returning to the sea and the palm-trees but she retained a perversely soft corner of her heart for the place that had welcomed her as a bride and educated her as a wife.

They settled smoothly into Weymouth life—or at least Jack did. Ruth and Bella had a hectic time of it for weeks, tripping over boxes and trying to sort out two households' furniture. But Jack, at his desk by the living-room window, was oblivious to the domestic chaos around him. As long as his meals arrived on time, well cooked (some things in a man's life don't ever change), he was content. With his books around him and typewriter to hand, he was soon back to work.

He already had a volume of poems called *A Different Drummer* ready for publication, so he turned instead to the revision of an allegory of which he had written the first immature draft nearly fifty years earlier in the emotional turmoil of losing little Barbara's company in 1938. He had re-written it in the late 1940s but no publisher would accept it, and when he went blind he gave up the struggle. Now the deadlock over his poetry drove him back to the old manuscript. He revised it again and sent it off under the title *The Shadowed Bed*. Jack describes it as 'a Calvinist allegory' set in a Cornish claywork village. It was a sweet moment when Lion Publishing accepted it for publication close on half a century after he had first penned it.

Jack continues to write poetry when the mood is upon him, when his imagination has been stimulated by a character he has read about in his Braille books or by exploring a new place. His method of composition remains the same as it has been for years. 'I suddenly become withdrawn,' he says, 'sealed off from ordinary thought-processes, inwardly watching for the appearance of words. One phrase follows another, linking and shaping until I can recognize whether the poem is to be in regular stanzas or

152

blank verse or irregular ode style or complex modern patterns. When the shape becomes clear I can begin to control it a little, rejecting some words and substituting others, but for the most part I simply look on and see the poem come to its full size in my mind. The tension relaxes, I am back in the everyday world, rummaging for pen and notebook so that I can write down what has pushed into my consciousness before I forget it. My most inspired poems need least revision—sometimes none at all.'

Novel-writing is not long behind him. As he says: 'No ideas or plots for stories ever come to me. They belong to a level which must be in contact with the external world of speech and action. I receive no impressions from which a story—even in verse—could germinate.'

Ruth does her best to keep him up to date with current events. She recounts to him the main news of the day and sometimes a scene by scene account of whatever she and Bella happen to be watching on television. For a man who has missed out on any direct experience of modern culture since just after the Coronation of Queen Elizabeth II in 1953, Jack keeps remarkably well informed. What is more, he forgets nothing. His memory is extraordinary. When Ruth has reported a piece of news to him, he files the information quietly away at the back of his mind and regularly astonishes her by being able to produce it months or even years later when she has forgotten all about it. If you ask Ruth for some detail of their past life, she will start to tell you and then, as likely as not, stop and say, 'Wait a moment. I'll just ask Jack. He'll know exactly.'

It is an unforgettable experience to watch them together, Ruth jerking his hand towards her to implant a question or a message, Jack listening gravely, his head bent forward before whispering a reply. Sometimes Ruth will slap his hand in mock-irritation and scribble, 'No, Jack—that's not what I meant', and repeat the question, her lips pursed, looking at him intently to see if he has understood this time.

What strikes most people who meet them for the first time is the fun they radiate. The pair of them giggle and flirt like teen-

153

agers. 'Bit skinny for your liking I was when I married you, eh Jack?' she scribbles, poking him none too gently in the right rib. He grins, a boyish, impish grin that lights up his whole face, and agrees, 'A bit bony. I had to make the best of it. I had to be patient'—and he lays a hand meaningfully on her now ample shoulder. 'Ooh, Jack, you are a one,' giggles Ruth and goes off into peals of laughter, her head shaking against his chest. He strokes her hair.

When they go out together, Ruth sustains an almost continuous commentary. Jack lets the impressions sink in silently. In public at least he rarely initiates conversation, but waits inscrutably in his private white universe for Ruth to tell him all he needs to know in order to function competently in her world. On a walk round the sub-tropical gardens at Abbotsbury in Dorset, for instance, Ruth will stop every few paces to give him a shorthand note of what she is seeing: 'Stream, Jack. Pool. High trees. Lovely doves, Jack . . . cooing. And look at these big blue rhododendrons, Jack.' He touches them: 'Hm, they're fluffy.' She guides his face into a clump of orange blossom. 'Smell, Jack. What does it make you think of?' 'Weddings,' says Jack, with his lovely smile.

So much of their conversation has to be shorthand. The rambling small-talk that forms the comfortable coinage of most marriages is a luxury they have to do without. Ruth cannot chirp away to him gaily about the hundred and one things that are crowding into her head. She can't chatter, as they walk, about running out of margarine and should she buy some on the way home and didn't Princess Diana look nice on the television but wasn't she getting thin. At least, she *could*, but it would take them two weeks to walk the length of Abbotsbury Gardens. Perhaps their biggest sacrifice in marriage has been the trivia of communication. When asked what the most frustrating thing was about not being able to talk directly to one another, Jack replied without hesitation: 'Only being able to say the important things, when there are hundreds of less important ones on your mind.'

But whatever Ruth does tell him goes deep. The intensity of

154

the sense-impressions that Jack receives, when mediated through the woman he loves, is striking. When Ruth guided him once on a summer's walk through a garden, not in Abbotsbury this time, but in Truro, her casual commentary prompted this poem: 'In a Truro Garden':

A summer hour of infinite scope,
Pulse and patchwork restful—path, mown slope,
Hot slant on neck, brow, right cheek or left
As I turn at her supple urge,
Then tunnel-feeling, eclipse, cool draught,
Stiff boughs scraping till we emerge.

We stoop at a sleepy pool's rim,
Touch wet stone—I fancy the gleam
Quiver, get quenched by cloud-shifts;
Then it's flower-shapes at my finger-ends—
Winged, grooved or studded: a petal lifts,
Rough and spongy, a smooth tip bends.

Now, higher up, we're in the orchard:
Pleasant to feel my forehead
Nudged by a living apple,
A fruit still fed among leaves,
In sight of the slim clear grey cathedral
Which answers the bad fruit—Eve's.

It's a spreading answer, we can tell:
The vines thrive here on the wall;
There's an unclogged scent, a sunning cat—
No scare from a serpent's hiss,
No sylvan treason. Across the flat
Flushed tongue of our city the spires spill bliss.

This is the same man who once wrote, with savage glee:

155

Praise God, the earth is maimed,
And there will be no daisies in that field
Next spring.

The poet has come full circle. So has the man. He sits contentedly
among fellow believers each Sunday in Weymouth Baptist
Church, the rebel who for years maintained a lonely Sabbath
vigil among the clay-tips, angrily despising the inadequacies of
ordinary Christian fellowship. Now in his seventies he is enjoying
the sense of restored balance, the sanity and the deep, deep
peace for which he always longed.

They sit together, Jack and Ruth, in their Weymouth sitting-
room; shoulder to shoulder, finger to palm, a couple who draw
their old-age pension but revel still in the fulfilment of a young
dream. Theirs now is the sunset dance that he celebrates in the
poem, 'A Different Drummer':

How does the misfit end? Is the young
Self-exile a waste? No, not this type.
Samaria makes reverence more subtly ripe,
Makes the shared dance at sunset—mine now—more vibrant.

They are dancing still.

Also published by Lion

The Shadowed Bed
by Jack Clemo

'Bert's face became dark and ugly, his arm jerked up—but it was not to strike. He pulled a red handkerchief from his pocket and wiped the blood from his cheek.'

In the Cornish claywork village of Carn Veor, sinister, occult forces are at work among the villagers. Over a single weekend, when the village is cut off from the outside world by a landslide, its conflicts reach flash-point. Then one of the characters central to the designs of evil is decisively released from its hypnotic hold over her.

In Jack Clemo's powerfully symbolic novel, the industrial scene takes on cosmic significance as the lives of the villagers are changed by warring magnetic forces.

'Clemo is the Bunyan of the century . . . He is about as easily digested as hot steel ingots; his power and importance cannot much longer be evaded.'
Kenneth Allsop

'One of the strangest and most original writers of our time.'
The Sunday Times

'Perhaps the last of the inspired, self-taught, English, working-class visionary writers.'
Charles Causley